THE
CONSUMERS UNION REPORT
ON
WINES AND SPIRITS

THE CONSUMERS UNION REPORT ON

Wines and Spirits

by the Editors of CONSUMER REPORTS

Consumers Union, Mount Vernon, New York

THE CONSUMERS UNION REPORT ON WINES AND SPIRITS is a special publication of Consumers Union, the nonprofit organization that publishes CONSUMER REPORTS, the monthly magazine of test reports, product Ratings, and buying guidance. Established in 1936, Consumers Union is chartered under the Not-For-Profit Corporation Law of the State of New York. The purposes of Consumers Union, as stated in its charter, are to provide consumers with information and counsel on consumer goods and services, to give information and assistance on all matters relating to the expenditure of the family income, and to initiate and to cooperate with individual and group efforts seeking to create and maintain decent living standards. Consumers Union derives its income solely from the sale of CONSUMERS REPORTS (magazine and TV) and other publications. CU accepts no advertising and is not beholden in any way to any commercial interest. Its Ratings and reports are solely for the information and use of the readers of its publications. Neither the Ratings nor the reports may be used in advertising or for any commercial purpose of any nature. Consumers Union will take all steps open to it to prevent or to prosecute any such uses of its materials or its name or the name of CONSUMERS REPORTS.

SECOND PRINTING, JUNE 1975
ALL RIGHTS RESERVED INCLUDING THE RIGHT OF
REPRODUCTION IN WHOLE OR IN PART IN ANY FORM
COPYRIGHT © 1972
BY CONSUMERS UNION OF UNITED STATES, INC.
MOUNT VERNON, NEW YORK
MANUFACTURED IN THE UNITED STATES OF AMERICA
LIBRARY OF CONGRESS CATALOG CARD NUMBER 72-90123
INTERNATIONAL STANDARD BOOK NUMBER 0-89043-001-2

A NOTE FROM CONSUMERS UNION
ON THE USE OF ALCOHOL

The vast majority of adult Americans who drink alcoholic beverages do so only occasionally or in moderation. For them the use of alcohol usually presents no problem. CU's evaluations in the field of wines and spirits, and our series of reports in CONSUMER REPORTS (the basis for this book) are designed to give those consumers buying guidance on what represents a significant segment of their expenditure.

At the same time, CU recognizes that alcohol is a toxic drug that, for some users, is addicting and may even be lethal. In a recent report to the Congress on "Alcohol and Health," the National Institute on Alcohol Abuse and Alcoholism estimated that five million Americans (about 5 per cent of the adult population) are "alcoholics"—alcohol addicts—while four million more (about 4 per cent) are alcohol abusers—problem drinkers. As used by them, alcohol can be considered a causal agent leading to more accidents, injuries, physical and mental illness, violence, crime, and death than any other drug.

Some users of alcoholic beverages find comfort in these statistics, for the odds against *their* becoming alcoholics would seem to be about 19 to 1. This is misleading, however, because users become addicts for biochemical, not statistical, reasons. For many, alcohol use is a kind of Russian Roulette, in which the user does not, and cannot, know in advance whether or when he will become addicted.

Understanding the effects of alcohol on the human system is basic to its moderate (and safe) use. "Alcohol in Perspective," an article published in the February 1967 issue of CONSUMER REPORTS, discussed these effects, including the dangers of combining alcohol with other drugs (particularly sedatives and tranquilizers). It also explained the significance of body weight on the absorption of alcohol, the equivalent effects of different alcoholic beverages (1½ ounces of 86-proof whiskey equals roughly 5 ounces of table wine or 1 pint of beer), and the intoxification levels of alcohol in the blood.

In addition, the article pointed out the early signs of problem drinking and cited various sources of help for both the potential and actual problem drinker. ("Alcohol in Perspective" is available as a reprint for 15 cents per copy—or $3.50 per 100—from Reprint Department, Consumers Union, Mount Vernon, N.Y. 10550.)

As a part of its continuing policy, CU advocates fundamental research and adequate education on the hazards of using *any* product—with adequate enforcement of workable laws governing misuse that endangers oneself or others. On both of these counts, when it comes to alcohol, much remains to be done.

Contents

INTRODUCTION

The main purpose of this book is to help you make wise decisions when you buy wines and spirits. Each section focuses on concrete brand-and-price buying guidance, based either on tastings of specific wines or liquors by a panel of experts or on the recommendations of CU's consultants. In addition, the book offers enough background information on each category of wines and spirits to help you make intelligent choices.

CU taste-tested those wines and spirits that may be expected to remain reasonably uniform from year to year and from bottle to bottle. On these, our buying advice comes to you, as usual, in the form of Ratings.* Wines in one category—still table wines—range so widely in type, availability, and price that we have provided for them not Ratings but Recommendations or Suggestions, based on the preferences and considered opinion of CU's wine consultants. (CU did taste-test three groups of modestly priced and widely available table wines—reds, whites, and rosés—to compare similar wines from several areas. The results of these tests, published in the October 1971, November 1971, and January 1972 issues of

---

*These Ratings were published by CONSUMER REPORTS in the period 1967–70. While they were, of course, based on wines and spirits purchased at the time of the tests, the comparisons of these branded products, which are consistently blended to a taste formula, should be currently valid, in the opinion of CU's consultants. Our only changes have been to eliminate products no longer available or no longer identifiable under the same brand name—and to update prices to June 1, 1972.

CONSUMER REPORTS, respectively, are included as an Appendix, pages 203-212.)

For our tastings we employed the discriminating noses and palates of experienced tasters—both professionals and distinguished amateurs. "Tasting," as used here, involves the interaction of many senses, far more than the simple reaction of the taste buds themselves. Our panels evaluated the clarity and depth of color, the strength and complexity of bouquet or aroma, and the many nuances of flavor—subtleties such as the body and dryness of a wine, the smokiness of a Scotch, the smoothness of a brandy. In some cases they compared these to standards set up by CU; in others to their own highly developed memory-image of a fine bordeaux, for example, or a true Bourbon. To make their evaluations as objective as possible, our experts did all their tasting "blind"—that is, with no identification save code numbers on the samples they were judging.

Taste preferences are, of course, highly subjective; there's no law that says your tastes must agree with our experts'. Indeed our panels did not always reach a consensus themselves. Still, you may find it instructive to learn what they liked—and why.

The chapter arrangement of the book follows what may be called a *natural* order. The first part covers wines, which are fundamentally products of fermentation, a process of nature in which alcohol is manufactured from sugars or starches through the agency of the enzymes in certain yeasts. Among the wines, we begin with the most natural—the still table wines—and end with those more complex in production, the fortified wines. The second part of the book deals with spirits, which are not only fermented but then distilled as well, a process that further concentrates the drink. Here, the first to be covered are the whiskies, brandies, and rums, to which nature still imparts a certain character. The last are the premixed cocktails and cocktail mixes, where the hand of man is most strongly evident.

It is not at all unlikely that you start this book with certain beliefs about wines and liquors that may be contradicted by CU's findings. Before you discount the findings, it might be worthwhile to try some blind tastings yourself. You can try this triangle test on any wine or spirit, but it is interesting to start with one you know (or think you know). Here's how to go about it. Get a bottle of your favorite wine or liquor and a bottle of another brand (if it's wine, get another of the same type, but one you think is far better or far worse). Have someone pour a little of one brand into a glass and a little of the other into two more glasses. You should not know which brand goes into which glass, but have your helper keep track. Then sip from each of the three glasses trying to judge which two contain the same brand, and, also, which you prefer. Since your chances of guessing right by sheer chance in any one test are one in three, you should repeat the procedure at least three times in a row. There is no need even to swallow as you taste. It is best to rinse your mouth with water between tastings. Some of CU's consultants were astonished at the results obtained from this procedure. You may be, too.

WINES

SUGGESTED WINE GLASSES

| All-purpose wine glass | All-purpose glass #2 | German wine glass | Champagne tulip |

A wine glass should be large enough to gather the bouquet properly. Either all-purpose glass is correct for any wine. These hold eight to ten ounces and, at serving time, should be filled no more than half way. The traditional German glass is often used for chilled whites or rosés. The champagne tulip is preferred to the showier saucer.

TYPICAL BOTTLE SHAPES

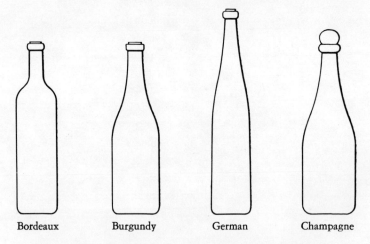

| Bordeaux | Burgundy | German | Champagne |

Though these traditional shapes originated in Europe, they are used by wine producers all over the world to bottle wines similar in character. For example, California producers put cabernet sauvignon in the bordeaux bottle, pinot noir in the burgundy. For German-style wines, the "flute" in brown indicates rhine wines; in green, moselles.

Chapter 1

WINES IN GENERAL

M an may have learned how to make wine even before he learned how to farm—as long ago, some think, as the Stone Age—for wine can be fermented readily from wild fruits and berries.

Here is a somewhat simplified description of the fermentation process. Take a sweet mixture—perhaps grape juice—and expose it to various yeasts that exist in the air and on the skins of the grapes (that waxlike bloom on ripe grapes is yeast). Soon these yeasts produce certain enzymes that trigger the conversion of the sugars in the mixture into liquid ethyl alcohol, and gaseous carbon dioxide which escapes (unless restrained, as it is in sparkling wines). This is fermentation, and it continues until all the sugar present has been used up or the alcoholic content has risen to about 14 per cent and thereby inhibited the yeasts—which, like all other living organisms, can tolerate only so much alcohol. When the fermenting ceases, you have wine—a raw wine perhaps, since it hasn't been aged or "fined" (clarified), but wine nonetheless.

Of course the defining element in wine isn't just ethyl alcohol. It contains in minute quantities a multitude of other substances: sugars, acids, essential oils, alcohols other than ethyl alcohol, and others. Some of these materials pass from the grape juice into the wine unchanged by fermentation; others emerge through fermentation and subsequent aging. From them all a wine derives its characteristic flavor, aroma, and color. Flavor and aroma vary from year to year as the quality of the grapes from which the wine is made varies; and, owing to many factors acting in combination—primarily the amount and timing of sunshine and rain—no two harvests from any one vineyard are ever quite alike. A viticulturist's days are not all wine and roses—he has his good years, but he has his bad years, too.

THE CLASSES OF WINE

Classified according to the way they are processed, wines fall into four broad categories.

Table wines

These are still—*i.e.,* nonsparkling—wines, and they come in red and rosé and white varieties. As we have noted, they are the most natural of wines, containing no added alcohol, no added flavorings, and usually no added sugar. They run from very dry* to quite sweet and present the widest range of variations among types, as well as the greatest likelihood of bottle-to-bottle variation within a given type. Their alcoholic content is generally from 10 to 14 per cent.

Sparkling wines

Of these, champagne is the best known, but nearly every wine-producing country makes a sparkling white wine (spumante from Italy and sekt from Germany are examples). There are, too, sparkling reds and rosés from many countries, including the popular Cold Duck from American producers. The traditional sparkling wines are naturally carbonated: The carbon dioxide produced by them during a secondary fermentation is kept under pressure instead of being allowed to escape. The sparkling wines range from rather dry to rather sweet and, like table wines, usually contain from 10 to 14 per cent alcohol.

Fortified wines

These include sherry, port, marsala, and others. They are called "for-

---

In wine terminology, "dry" is the opposite of "sweet" and will be so used throughout this book.

tified" because their alcoholic content is boosted above its natural upper limit of 14 per cent to 16 to 21 per cent by adding wine spirits (brandy).

There are both red and white fortified wines (though some look rather brown), and they range from very dry to very sweet. The brandy is added to some of them after they have fermented, yielding dry wines; with others alcohol is added during fermentation, so that the process is arrested and unfermented sugar is left in the wine, yielding sweet wines.

Flavored, or aromatized, wines

These wines, too, are fortified with extra alcohol, so that their total alcoholic content usually ranges from 15½ to 20 per cent. They are also flavored with herbs, barks, berries, or whatever flavoring agents their "secret formulas" call for. Vermouths, both dry and sweet, are flavored wines, and so are the many red and white aperitif wines.

SHOPPING FOR WINE

Where you can buy wine and spirits varies from state to state. In one, you buy wine in grocery stores but spirits in drug stores; in another, spirits and fortified wines in liquor stores but table wines in the supermarket; in yet another, anything alcoholic in state-controlled stores only. In some states, liquor stores are forbidden to sell anything but alcoholic beverages; in others they can sell snack foods; in still others they can sell decanters, corkscrews, and such accessories.

The most important distinction, for wine shoppers, is between the so-called "control" states, in which a state agency actually controls the stores, and the private-enterprise states. The state-control store usually offers the buyer only the lowest common denominator— merchandise with the widest acceptance. It cannot cater to individual taste, dabble in small quantities, or buy from experimental producers. It sticks to the standards, so your chances of finding something unusual are not great. The store may special-order, often in case lots only, particularly if you know what you want and pay for it in advance. On the other hand, because they are buying in such large quantities, for statewide distribution, their prices for standard products are, on occasion, lower than non-control states.

Even after you have absorbed all the information in this book and are out shopping with notations from our Ratings or Recommendations, you may still be fair game for a sharp wine salesman. For one thing, as we've noted, the quality of a particular wine may vary from year to year, especially if it's from France or Germany. For another, because of the almost unlimited number of wines available, our guidance often comes to you in lists of "Recommended Shippers," only a few of which will be carried in any one store.

The result is that you will often have to rely on the honesty and intelligence of the wine merchant you're dealing with. How can you judge him? Here are some questions to ask yourself: Does he keep his corked bottles of fine wine resting on their sides so the cork will stay wet and tight? Does he keep his wines neatly arranged by category so you can easily find what you're looking for? Do your knowledgeable wine friends recommend him? Has anyone you know tried to return an off-bottle for exchange or refund? Does he give discounts on case purchases? (There is a practice among wine distributors of offering retail dealers "post-offs," or discounts, on case purchases. These savings can be passed along to the consumer.)

A wine dealer who meets these qualifications can do a great deal more than locate a bottle of wine for which you already have the name. He can guide you to substitutes when your choice is not available. He can warn you when a wine of good repute falls below its standard. He can suggest new wines for you to try, wines that he or other customers have found a particularly good value. He can let you know when he is to receive limited shipments of wines he knows you like. If his store is large enough, he may have wines bottled and labeled under his own name, and from such a knowledgeable dealer, they may indeed be worth trying. This is good business for him, but you benefit too—better wines at lower prices.

Chapter 2

TABLE WINES

In an earlier book on this subject, in 1963, Consumers Union noted that more people from more and more countries were drinking European—in particular, French—wines and that the prices of these wines were, in consequence, soaring higher and higher. Today, in some instances, they have soared practically out of sight. If a bottle of "great" table wine used to be expensive, a new word ought to be coined to describe what it costs now. And the fact is that scarcity—not quality—is mainly responsible for this state of affairs.

CU's RECOMMENDATIONS

Small wonder, then, that one of the tasks we set our consultants was to find European table wines of superior quality that were not so acutely affected by the law of supply and demand that their cost to the consumer had become exorbitant. Moreover, we urged them to find, if they could, a number of such wines so that if a particular brand wasn't available in your locality possibly another would be. Finally, we told them to round up some good American table wines, which generally cost less than the imports. The results of their efforts may be found in Chapters 3, 4, and 5.

Of the thousands of domestic and imported table wines distributed in the United States, our consultants chose some 700 to recommend. Most of the others they considered were judged unworthy of mention, but some, every bit as good as those cited, were not listed because their distribution was limited. On the other hand, some reputedly exceptional but sparsely distributed wines were mentioned for those lucky enough to be where they can be found.

You will also discover among the Recommendations—heading them, in fact—wines whose prices range from high to astronomical. These are, by and large, the "great" and "outstanding" wines that for generations have been a standard of excellence for the industry. Even though you probably wouldn't think of buying them, you should at least be familiar with them. It is unlikely that, if you are an average wine drinker, you would discern whatever quality differences there might be between an "outstanding" $10 wine (which may not be at all ready to drink) and a "very good" inexpensive wine—so why buy the former?

There is enough choice among our Recommendations of wines, so that our consultants feel you should have little trouble finding several that will please you. In fact, you may actually prefer some of the so-called modest wines to their august rivals. Or an American wine to a European wine. And if you should, you owe apologies to no one. We cannot overemphasize this point: The final arbiter in wine-buying—as in tie-buying, dress-buying, wallpaper-buying—is and should be your own taste.

VINTAGES

There's something else besides long lists of high prices that won't be found in the next three chapters, and that is the usual to-do over vintage-labeling. A great deal of confusion has arisen over the misleading phrase "vintage wine." There is a "vintage" (the harvest at a vineyard) *every* year, and whenever all the wine (or nearly all, depending on local laws) in a particular bottle comes from grapes harvested in a particular year, the producer has the right to put the year on the label—and he usually does. This may or may not indicate anything about the quality of the wine. In Italy, Spain, and California, where climate and weather are relatively consistent, year-labeling is not of great consequence. But the contrary is true in France and Germany—as the price tags of wine of "great" years vividly attest. It should also be pointed out that the effect of climate and weather on grapes varies from district to district and, in some cases, from vineyard to vineyard *within* a district. The upshot is that some year-labeled wines are better than those not so labeled—and some aren't. As a result, you will find few references to specific years in the chapters that follow.

Champagne is an exception. Champagne is year-labeled only when all climate conditions have acted together to produce a harvest of superior grapes. "Vintage" champagne is, therefore, always of special quality (and more expensive) than non-vintage of the same brand. This practice may well have given rise to the confusion over the term "vintage wine." The same is true of port.

Incidentally, when you do see a year on a bottle, you can learn at least one meaningful detail from it: the age of the wine. CU's consultants advise drinking most white and rosé wines while they are young, between one and three years old. On the other hand, most quality red wines improve with age, up to a point—try to drink them between their third and eighth years. Some very fine red wines can benefit from much longer aging (and indeed some *require* aging to be drinkable)—but only if they are well stored.

STORAGE

In storage, the dangers to a bottle of table wine are air, heat, and light. Air entering the bottle (because the cork has dried out and no longer makes a tight fit) may bring on bacterial activity that can turn the wine into vinegar. (No problem here with screw-capped bottles.) Excessive heat can ruin a wine's flavor (and so, to a lesser degree, can prolonged, excessive cold), and too much light can make it cloudy or dull-looking.

A bottle of table wine, then, should be stored on its side in a dark place where the temperature does not fluctuate widely or rapidly from 55° F. Since most homeowners, let alone apartment dwellers, can't manage this condition, it would seem that the wise course for the majority of wine drinkers is to do no long-term storing—particularly of white wines, which are even more sensitive to heat than are red. However, if a good value in a case of red wine comes your way, don't pay too much attention to what we have just said, for red wine left undisturbed—unjostled—in a dark closet has been known to survive some fairly warm summers. Just be sure that it isn't subjected to sudden, sharp changes of temperature.

SERVING WINE

CU's consultants suggest that you chill your white or rosé wines to 40° to 50° before you serve them. An hour or two in the refrigerator (not the freezer) or twenty minutes in an ice bucket will do the job. (The time will depend on the temperature at which they were stored.) Red table wines should be served at near room temperature; if they have been stored in a cool place, they should be allowed to sit out (in an upright position) until they have warmed to roughly 65° F. Of course, if *you* wish, you can chill these, too, the experts concede (though *they* wouldn't).

Red wines should be uncorked about an hour before you serve them in order to let them "breathe" and thus enhance their bouquet. Very young wines could benefit from longer-than-normal breathing time. However, very old bottles must be opened with caution, decanted, and served almost immediately—many would fade and deteriorate if left to breathe by the usual rules.

Before you uncork any bottle, first strip the protective foil well away from its mouth so the wine won't pick up a metallic taste. Then extract the cork and wipe the bottle's lip inside and out. CU's consultants say that air- or gas-pressured cork extractors do not harm the wine. Among the more conventional types of corkscrews, they like best those that have good leverage and a long, round-wire screw, rather than a sharp-edged cast screw.

Unless yours is a very formal household, our consultants see no reason for you to have both red-wine and white-wine glasses. One size should do nicely for all table and sparkling wines. The size they recommend is 8 or 9 ounces, in clear, colorless tulip-shaped stemware. Filled halfway at most, so that the empty portion can collect the wine's bouquet, a glass of this size will provide a generous serving. Though many find the thinner glasses more agreeable for wine drinking, you can probably find similar glasses in sturdier commercial versions if you're worried about breakage. (See page 14 for suggested glasses.)

At about 4 ounces a serving, you will get about six glasses from a European bottle, which may look like a fifth but usually contains only around 23 or 24 fluid ounces. An American wine bottle *is* a fifth: It holds 25.6 fluid ounces. European or American, two bottles are still what you'll need for a dinner for four if everybody wants a refill. If there's some wine left over, recork the bottle firmly, put it into the refrigerator (whether it's white or red), and drink what remains of it soon—within a week at the outside.

In a restaurant the wine waiter will pour a little for the host's approval, before serving the guests, but in your own home, you should take this step earlier, on opening the bottle. This taste allows you to judge whether the wine is sound and to pick up any stray bits of cork. Once in a while, alas, the wine won't be sound. It will be sour or "corky"—that is, it will have been spoiled because of a defective cork. If you can, have a spare bottle available, just in case. In serving wine, the host should pour each glass in turn, proceeding from his left clockwise around the table. Do not wrap the bottle— this is simply an affectation and prevents your guests from learning about the wine from its label. If you're worried about dripping, a slight twist as you end each pour should prevent it.

WINING OUT

The same bottles for which you'd pay $2 to $5 in a wine shop will cost you from $3 to $10 in a restaurant—and sometimes the mark-up is steeper yet. For this reason you should shop the wine list with care. Until you become a knowledgeable wine buyer, don't use restaurant meals as an occasion to broaden your experience—it will be an expensive way to learn. Many restaurants have poor storage facilities, and many have a poor range of selections. (By "poor" we don't necessarily mean the reverse of "extensive," for some small restaurants that list no more than four or five wines offer excellent choices.)

What we suggest, then, is that you hold yourself back, particularly when you visit a restaurant unfamiliar to you. Unless you spot a wine with which you are well acquainted—in which case you

Wines by the Jug

One obvious way to cut down your wine-drinking costs is to buy wine by the gallon, or at least by the half-gallon. The same wine (Almadén's Mountain Red Claret, for example) that lists at $1.59 a fifth costs only $5.31 for the gallon, a clear saving of $2.64 over the five-fifths price. There are two drawbacks to this apparently simple maneuver. First of all, the wines available in larger-than-fifth bottles are for the most part limited to what might be called the *vins ordinaires*, the everyday wines. Many of these are good, honest, very drinkable wines, but you have to realize that your savings will generally be limited to this category. Many California and New York wines and some imports (Spanish and Italian wines, primarily) are offered in half-gallon and gallon sizes, and we note this in our Recommendations with the use of a star (★) by the wine name. The second problem with half-gallon and gallon jugs is storage. Once a bottle has been opened, the air in the bottle (no matter how well capped or corked) will cause the wine to deteriorate. This process can be retarded by storing the bottle in the refrigerator until used again. Chilling is no problem with whites, which you want to serve cold anyway, but it means that if you like your reds at room temperature, you have to bring the bottle out almost two hours before the meal. A more satisfactory solution is to decant the wine, as soon as you open it, into scrupulously clean fifth or quart bottles, preferably of the screw-cap variety. These should be tightly capped and can be refrigerated or not, depending on how soon you expect to use the wine.

know pretty much what you're getting and about how much you can expect to pay (about twice the retail price)—try the less expensive wines. If there are only two of you, perhaps a half-bottle will be enough. These average out at a higher price per ounce, but of course you will actually pay out less. More and more restaurants are now offering wines by the glass or in carafes of various sizes. The wine served you in this manner is usually an inexpensive jug wine or house brand, but it can often be quite pleasant, and risks the least cash outlay.

If you're planning to order wine with your meal at a restaurant, get the wine list with the menu and make your choice at that time. If you order a red, have it brought to the table and opened; if you order a white, make sure that it is already chilled or put into an ice bucket for chilling. In either case you will have ensured that you have the wine of your choice in its best drinking condition when your food arrives. The waiter should show you the bottle so that you can check the label and make sure it is the exact wine you ordered. In an expensive restaurant you may find yourself consulting with a wine steward, or *sommelier,* and it is usual to add a dollar or two as a tip for his advice and service.

EUROPEAN AND AMERICAN VITICULTURE

If wine-merchandising is becoming a trifle overheated, wine-making and grape-growing for the most part still follow the old and honorable traditions, and these go back a long, long way. Grapes have always grown well and abundantly in Europe and Asia Minor, and so grape wines have been made and drunk in these regions since ancient times.

From the varieties of grapes indigenous to these parts of the world, man, through selection and improvement, eventually developed what are now known as the European *vitis vinifera* varieties. Each of these varieties, whether red or white, has its own distinctive characteristics, which alter somewhat from region to region and country to country, depending on the growing conditions. In the world of wines, nothing is more confusing than the names of the wines themselves. From country to country—and even from region to region within a country—the nomenclature varies. For the beginner, an understanding of geography can be a great help, for, in very general terms, it can be said that the smaller the area producing the wine, the better the wine.

In France, for example, two large and important geographical *regions* producing wine are Bordeaux and Burgundy. Within these regions are *districts;* within each district are *communes* or parishes (we would call them towns or villages); and within these communes are *vineyards*. As you move down this geographical scale, the wines become progressively finer. Wine labeled simply *Vin rouge* from France is made of grapes grown anywhere in the country. *Vin de Bordeaux* on a label would normally be better, and *Médoc* (one of the Bordeaux districts) even better. *Pauillac* is one of the communes in the Médoc district, and on a label would usually indicate very good wine. Even finer would be château-bottled wine from one of the vineyards within the commune of Pauillac, with Château Latour or Château Lafite-Rothschild at the very top of the list. Here you would reach what are considered two of the finest wines in the world, made from grapes grown in vineyards of no more than 140–150 acres.

While this equation—geography = quality—cannot be applied without some qualification, it does give you a starting point, particularly for the major European wine-producing countries—France, Germany, and Italy—in which the laws governing the production of wine and its labeling have gradually become codified over the years.

American wines have their own history. Settlers in the eastern United States, particularly New York State and Ohio, started early-on to make wine from native grapes; but these grapes (*vitis labrusca* for the most part) are a wholly different species from *vitis vinifera,* and the wines from them bear no more than passing resemblance to European wines. *Vitis vinifera* vines, however, have taken very kindly to the climate of California. (In fact, toward the end of the last century, after an unintentionally imported American grape louse had all but ruined many of the vineyards of Europe, *vitis vinifera* vines resistant to that louse were brought back from California and succeeded in reestablishing the stock.) All the same, California wines, though related, are not identical to their European counterparts.

Recent viticultural developments have proven that some vinifera vines, particularly chardonnay and riesling, can also flourish in New York State's climate. Some of these wines, of exceptional quality, are already available on a commercial scale and are now offered in some wine shops and restaurants.

A new American approach

Many American producers have begun to stress the differences between wines of the Old and the New Worlds. In some instances, instead of building up unfounded expectations by calling their products claret, chablis, sauterne, or other names of European origin, they have begun to name them after the grape variety that predominates in their production. These *varietal* wines, as they are called, bear such names as cabernet sauvignon or pinot noir, for example, rather than claret or burgundy; riesling instead of rhine; or semillon instead of sauternes. A varietal name is no blanket guarantee of quality, but CU's consultants believe that, on the whole, the producers tend to prepare their varietal wines with more care than they give to their generically named wines—and the varietals do begin with better grapes.

How do U.S. wines compare with European wines? CU's consultants believe that some domestic wines, though no match for Europe's greatest, can hold their own with some very fine European wines. And they say that, at the other end of the scale, in the everyday wines, U.S. producers often do a better job than their European counterparts. In this connection, we call your attention again to the Appendix reprint of results of the tastings in which American wines were compared with similar European wines.

In the lists of Recommendations of table wines in the next three chapters, the wines or producers are given in alphabetical order unless otherwise noted. The price ranges given are for the standard bottle (a full fifth from American producers, slightly less from most foreign producers). These ranges are representative prices at retail in New York State as of June 1, 1972.

~~~~~~

Chapter 3

RED WINES

Red wines can be made only from red grapes, for the color comes from the skins which are allowed to stay in the fermenting vats for periods varying from a few days up to two or even three weeks. Of course, the wine gets more than just color from the skins, and so the character of red wine is substantially different from that of white. While red table wines range from light to full-bodied and have an immense variety of tastes, nearly all can be characterized as "dry." Some, however, taste less dry than others, and if you like a fruitier, softer wine, you may prefer the burgundies to the more austere bordeaux, and, in Italian wines, the softer bardolinos or valpolicellas to the chiantis.

Judged by worldwide production, red wines are more popular than whites. From the American consumer's point of view, the important producing countries are France, Italy, Spain, and the United States. CU's consultants have listed Recommendations from each country, plus suggested reds available from other countries.

RED WINES OF FRANCE

The most famous French reds come from the regions of Bordeaux and Burgundy. The greatest of those can be very, very expensive, but there are still some our consultants classified as "very good" that are selling at reasonable prices. And it is possible to find even better values in some of the lesser-known red-wine districts—the Rhône, for example.

Red bordeaux (clarets)

A large and productive wine region of southwestern France, Bordeaux embraces several seaports, chief among which is the city of Bordeaux. Trade has always been brisk between these ports and England, where centuries ago Bordeaux reds became known as clarets. (The word was derived from the French *clairet*, or "light" —the wines were once lighter in color than they are today.)

The best bordeaux are produced, primarily from varieties of the cabernet grape, in four of Bordeaux's five main districts: Médoc, Graves, St. Émilion, and Pomerol. (The fifth district is Sauternes, noted for its white wine.) Bordeaux from the Graves district are fuller-bodied and less delicate than most of those of the Médoc. The wines of St. Émilion and Pomerol are still more full-bodied, some being nearly as robust as the red wines of Burgundy.

Châteaux wines

The distinctive characteristics of the wines from the different districts show up most clearly in the wines bottled on the property of the leading châteaux, as wine estates in Bordeaux are called. Some of these vineyards do, in fact, have a château (castle) on them. Others can boast of little more than sheds. The majority fall somewhere between the two extremes.

Of the more than two thousand châteaux of Bordeaux (including those that produce white wines), some two hundred have been classified, or ranked, at one time or another. Probably the most decisive classification resulted from the wine-tasting for the Paris Exposition of 1855, which ranked the presumably top sixty-two châteaux of Médoc and twenty-four of Sauternes. A hundred years passed before the outstanding châteaux of St. Émilion were officially rated. Pomerol is still to be officially classified. But all these classifications and reclassifications, however meaningful they once were or still may be, are not gospel. In the first place, it is the nature of château-bottled wines to vary. They are the product of a single vineyard and a single year, and some years are bound to be better

Petits Châteaux

The many small, relatively little known châteaux and minor growths vary considerably in the quality of their wines. Being little known, they *sometimes* offer exceptional values and *always* the excitement of the chase. The list below includes only a few of the wines which our consultants have found of good quality; there are many others. The following *petits châteaux* range in price from $2.25 to $4.

Ch. d'Agassac (Haut-Médoc), Ch. Bel-Orme (Haut-Médoc), Ch. Canteranne (St. Émilion), Ch. Capet-Guiller (St. Émilion), Ch. de Carignan (Premières Côtes de Bordeaux), Ch. Cissac (Haut-Médoc), Ch. Fonreaud (Haut-Médoc), Ch. Greysac (Haut-Médoc), Ch. Guiraud Cheval Blanc (Côtes de Bourg), Ch. La Tour Bicheau (Graves), Ch. Lassègue (St. Émilion), Ch. Lauretan (Premières Côtes de Bordeaux), Ch. Les Pradines (St. Estèphe), Ch. de Malleret (Haut-Médoc), Ch. Monbousquet (St. Émilion), Ch. Picque-Cailloux (Graves), Ch. Quinsac (Premières Côtes de Bordeaux), Ch. Respide (Graves), Ch. Sémeillan (Haut-Médoc), Ch. Sénéjac (Haut-Médoc), Ch. Toinet-Fombrauge (St. Émilion), Ch. Vieux Robin (Médoc).

—or worse—than others. But also, as we know, products may improve or worsen in quality even while their official reputations remain unchanged.

In the opinion of CU's consultants—and in the official classifications of red bordeaux wines—there are eight châteaux that rank as the "greatest." Four are in the Médoc district—Lafite-Rothschild, Latour, Margaux, and Mouton-Rothschild. Two are in St. Émilion —Ausone and Cheval-Blanc; one is in Graves—Haut-Brion; and one is in Pomerol—Pétrus. For these wines in good years, prices would start around $15 a bottle; even in off years (some might say "undrinkable"), the price would be around $8. It should be made very clear to beginners in the wine field that these great wines do not mature for many years. They may be at their best fifteen or twenty or more years after being bottled. A good wine merchant will not sell you a great château wine in its young years as "ready to drink." It is interesting to note that a young "great" bordeaux of a good year, a 1964 Château Lafite-Rothschild did not fare well in CU's 1971 taste-tests, almost certainly because it had not yet begun to show the full characteristics of a great wine. (See Appendix, page 205.)

The authenticity of a château wine is legally established on the label by the words *mis en bouteilles au château* (bottled at the château). Do not be misled by other phrases on bordeaux wines—they have no standing and mean only what the bottler wants them to mean.

SOME RECOMMENDED RED BORDEAUX CHÂTEAUX WINES

The following châteaux wines have been graded by CU's consultants into four quality categories. The price ranges given are for good years in which there is an average yield. For the rare "great" years or for years when the yield is low, the prices may well run higher. The district or commune is given in parentheses after each château.

Outstanding ($7 to $12): Ch. Beychevelle (St. Julien), Ch. Brane-Cantenac (Margaux), Ch. Cos d'Estournel (St. Estèphe), Domaine de Chevalier (Graves), Ch. Ducru-Beaucaillou (St. Julien), Ch. Gruaud-Larose (St. Julien), Ch. La Mission-Haut-Brion (Graves), Ch. Lascombes (Margaux), Ch. Léoville-Las-Cases (St. Julien), Ch. Léoville-Poyferré (St. Julien), Ch. Montrose (St. Estèphe), Ch. Palmer (Margaux), Ch. Pape-Clément (Graves), Ch. Pichon-Longueville (Baron) (Pauillac), Ch. Pichon-Longueville (Comtesse de Lalande) (Pauillac), Ch. Rausan-Ségla (Margaux), Ch. Rauzan-Gassies (Margaux), Ch. Talbot (St. Julien).

Excellent ($5 to $8): Ch. l'Angélus (St. Émilion), Ch. Batailley (Pauillac), Ch. Bouscaut (Graves), Ch. Branaire-Ducru (St. Julien), Ch. Calon-Ségur (St. Estèphe), Ch. Canon (St. Émilion), Ch. Cantemerle (Haut-Médoc), Ch. Cantenac-Brown (Margaux), Clos Fourtet (St. Émilion), Ch. Duhart-Milon-Rothschild (Pauillac), Ch. Durfort-Vivens (Margaux), Ch. Figeac (St. Émilion), Ch. la Gaffelière (St. Émilion), Ch. Giscours (Margaux), Ch. Haut-Batailley (Pauillac), Ch. d'Issan (Margaux), Ch. Lynch-Bages (Pauillac), Ch. Malescot-St.-Exupéry (Margaux), Ch. Mouton-Baron-Philippe (Pauillac), Ch.

Nenin (Pomerol), Ch. Pavie (St. Émilion), Ch. Pontet-Canet (Pauillac), Ch. Prieuré-Lichine (Margaux), Ch. Trotanoy (Pomerol), Ch. Vieux-Château-Certan (Pomerol).

Very Good ($4 to $7): Ch. Belair (St. Émilion), Ch. Boyd-Cantenac (Margaux), Ch. Canon-la-Gaffelière (St. Émilion), Ch. Carbonnieux (Graves), Ch. Croizet-Bages (Pauillac), Ch. l'Évangile (Pomerol), Ch. Gazin (Pomerol), Ch. Gloria (St. Julien), Ch. Grand-Puy-Lacoste (Pauillac), Ch. Haut-Bailly (Graves), Ch. Kirwan (Margaux), Ch. Lafon-Rochet (St. Estèphe), Ch. La Lagune (Haut-Médoc), Ch. La Tour-Carnet (Haut-Médoc), Ch. Magdelaine (St. Émilion), Ch. Marquis-de-Terme (Margaux), Ch. de Pez (St. Estèphe), Ch. Phélan-Ségur (St. Estèphe), Ch. Ripeau (St. Émilion), Ch. Rouget (Pomerol).

Good ($3.50 to $6): Ch. l'Arrosée (St. Émilion), Ch. Chasse-Spleen (Haut-Médoc), Ch. Dassault (St. Émilion), Ch. Larmande (St. Émilion), Ch. La Tour-Martillac (Graves), Ch. de Marbuzet (St. Estèphe), Ch. Meyney (St. Estèphe), Ch. Pédesclaux (Pauillac), Ch. St. Georges (St. Émilion), Ch. Siran (Haut-Médoc), Ch. Trimoulet (St. Émilion), Ch. Troplong-Mondot (St. Émilion).

Shipper blends

Actually, most of the exported bordeaux wine is neither very good nor very bad, for most of it is not château-bottled but sold in casks to wine shippers, who blend it into uniform, ready to drink, never great but never poor bottles of eminently drinkable wine.

There are two types of shipper blends: those from a specific geographical area (commune or district) and *monopole* blends (which use a shipper's own proprietary name). The shipper may also put his special trade-name on a commune or district blend, but it will always have the district or commune name too. The better blends, in the opinion of CU's consultants, are generally those from a particular commune; next in line come those from the district, a larger area. Many of these communes and districts have established histories of producing good wine. The four main districts and some of the more important communes are given on page 35, with price ranges for their wines. The name of the district or commune will normally be in the largest type on the label, but you can always double-check where the wine is from by looking for the *Appellation Contrôlée* (see next page).

Appellation Contrôlée

Appellation Contrôlée is the French government's "Sterling" mark. Most people think it is simply a geographic designation—that is, *Appellation Médoc Contrôlée* would only guarantee that the wine is from the Médoc district of Bordeaux—but actually it signifies much more, a quality control of sorts. It means that the grapes used for the wine are the approved grapes for that wine, that the grape-growing and wine-making methods are the approved methods, and that the legal quantity of wine permitted for the vineyard or area has been carefully adhered to. A notch below the *Appellation Contrôlée* imprimatur is the *V.D.Q.S.* designation (it stands for *Vins Délimités de Qualité Supérieure*). This is used on the label of wines from certain lesser regions in France, but it is still a mark of quality since its use is well regulated. If you don't find either of these designations on a bottle of wine from France, don't buy it. It *may* be good but you have nothing to go by.

As monopole brands are usually blends of wines from any part of the Bordeaux region, this would, of course, include areas not always noted for the high quality of their wines. Monopoles, despite their impressive names and arresting labels, are a bit cheaper than district blends—but even so are not usually as good values, according to CU's consultants. You can generally recognize a monopole since it will normally be labeled *Appellation Bordeaux Contrôlée*. Bottles marked *Bordeaux Supérieur* should be a little better than those labeled simply *Bordeaux*. But look out for such glittery nonsense as *mis en bouteilles dans nos chais* (bottled in our warehouse). The shipper has to do his blending and bottling somewhere. The phrase means nothing—certainly not that the wine was château-bottled. Other phrases you may see on labels, with a similar lack of standing, are: *mis en bouteilles dans nos caves* (bottled in our cellars); *mis en bouteilles en Bordeaux* (bottled in Bordeaux); and *grand vin* (great wine).

To guide you in buying both types of shipper blends, CU's consultants have recommended below, in addition to the wines from Bordeaux's finer communes and districts, a group of reliable shippers who blend from these areas. Many of these same shippers have their own monopole blends, a few of which are listed as "Suggestions" on page 36. Not all these shippers have wide distribution, but you should find a representation of them in any reasonably well-stocked wine store.

SOME RECOMMENDED
RED BORDEAUX COMMUNE WINES

The following communes, all in the Médoc district, are considered by CU's consultants to produce the better wines at this level. If possible, select a commune blend from one of the shippers recommended below.

Good ($2.50 to $5): Margaux, Pauillac, St. Estèphe, St. Julien.

SOME RECOMMENDED
RED BORDEAUX DISTRICT WINES

CU's consultants suggest looking for the following district names. In choosing a district wine, the shipper's name (below) becomes an even more important element in the decision.

Good ($2.25 to $5): Haut-Médoc, Médoc, Pomerol, St. Émilion.

SOME RECOMMENDED
SHIPPERS OF RED BORDEAUX WINES

The following list of shippers recommended by our consultants should be used as a general guide only, since it must be based on a judgment of the overall quality of the shipper's wines. Your own selections could well be influenced by a wine merchant's recommendations or your own tasting.

Good: B & G (Barton & Guestier), Calvert & Cie, Chanson Père & Fils, Domaine Cordier, Cruse & Fils Frères, Th. Darriet & Co., Dourthe Frères, F. Ginestet, N. Johnston & Fils, T. Jouvet & Cie, Ed. Kressman, Lavergne, A. de Luze & Fils, Schröder & Schyler, Sichel & Fils Frères, Tytell & Fils.

SOME SUGGESTED
RED BORDEAUX MONOPOLE BLENDS

The following shippers' trade-named blends, ranging in price from $2 to $4, are entitled to the *Bordeaux,* or *Bordeaux Supérieur, Appellation Contrôlée:* Club Claret (A. de Luze & Fils), Cordon de Bordeaux (Chanson Père & Fils), Grand Chartrons (N. Johnston & Fils), Lion Rouge (Calvet & Cie), Monopole Rouge (Cruse & Fils Frères), Monopole Rouge (Ed. Kressman), Mouton Cadet (La Bergerie), Pavillon Rouge de Bordeaux (Lavergne), Prince Noir (Barton & Guestier), Plaisir de France (Cordier).

Red burgundies

The finest red wines of Burgundy, in eastern France, come from the Côte d'Or district. They are made from the pinot noir grape and are considered the only "true" burgundies. Beaujolais is another district in Burgundy, but its wines, from the gamay grape, are different from those of the Côte d'Or and will be discussed separately. (Of Burgundy's three other districts, Chablis produces only white wines, Maconnais is noted mainly for its whites, and the Chalonnais produces lesser wines, both red and white, many of them sparkling.)

Estate-bottled burgundies

Most of the finest red burgundies are "estate bottled," the Burgundian equivalent of the Bordeaux château-bottling system. The label of an estate-bottled wine will read either *mis au domaine, mis en bouteilles au domaine,* or *mis en bouteilles par le propriétaire,* all of which mean, in essence, that the wine was made and bottled on the estate by the owner. In the judgment of CU's consultants, the greatest estate-bottled burgundies are (in alphabetical order): Bonnes Mares, Chambertin, Chambertin-Clos de Beze, Grands-Échezeaux, Musigny, Richebourg, Romanée-Conti, and La Tâche. Like their bordeaux counterparts, these wines are so scarce and in such demand that their prices bear little relation even to their high quality. For good years, you will have to pay from $15 to over $30 a bottle.

The Wines of Hospices de Beaune

Hospices de Beaune is one of the best-known names in Burgundy. Through the centuries this ancient hospital has been donated parts of vineyards by generous patrons, so that today its many small, choice holdings are scattered about the Côte d'Or. It is difficult for the neophyte wine buyer to judge a Hospices de Beaune wine, however, for it isn't labeled with the name of the commune or vineyard from which it comes. Instead it bears the name of its donor. For example, *Hospices de Beaune, Cuvée Charlotte Dumay* denotes wine from the holdings bestowed by Charlotte Dumay; these happen to be in the renowned commune of Aloxe-Corton. The prestige associated with the Hospices de Beaune wines affects the prices—they are usually a little more expensive than comparable burgundies.

Unlike the châteaux, however, which are typically owned by one family (or one group or corporation), the vineyards of Burgundy are usually divided among many owners. The famous Clos de Vougeot, for instance, is owned by over sixty persons. That doesn't mean all of them make an individual wine: Some have their holdings managed for them; some sell their wine in casks to shippers for blending with other wines from Clos de Vougeot. (See comments on shippers' blends.) But many of the owners do make and bottle their own wine. When you decide to buy a particular estate-bottled Clos de Vougeot, you will undoubtedly be getting a very fine wine. However, it may not be an exact replica of a Clos de Vougeot you've had before.

The vineyard holdings in Burgundy have not been subject to rigid classification like the châteaux of Bordeaux, but thirty-one vineyards are ranked as *grand cru* (great growth) and entitled to their own *Appellation Contrôlée,* as, for example, the eight "greatest" burgundies listed earlier. The vineyards of the next step down, the *premier cru* (first growth), have on their labels the name of the vineyard plus the name of the commune in which they are located, but the *Appellation Contrôlée* will be that of the commune. For example, a wine named *Pommard Les Épenots* is from the vineyard of Les Épenots (a *premier cru*) in the commune of Pommard, and somewhere on the label it will say *Appellation Pommard Contrôlée*.

SOME RECOMMENDED ESTATE-BOTTLED RED BURGUNDY WINES

CU's consultants have ranked the following estate-bottled wines into four quality groups. Most of these are from *grand cru* vineyards; some are from *premier cru*.

Outstanding ($7 to $20): Beaune Les Grèves, Le Corton, Clos de la Roche, Clos de Vougeot, Gevrey-Chambertin Clos St. Jacques, Gevrey-Chambertin La Grande Rue, Latricières-Chambertin, La Romanée, Romanée-St. Vivant.

Excellent ($6 to $15): Chambolle-Musigny Les Amoureuses, Beaune Clos des Mouches, Beaune Les Fèves, Charmes-Chambertin, Corton-Bressandes, Corton-Clos du Roi, Échezeaux, Mazis-Chambertin, Nuits St. Georges Les Porrets, Nuits-St. Georges Les St. Georges, Vosne-Romanée Les Malconsorts.

Very Good ($5 to $12): Clos de Tart, Clos St. Denis, Pommard Les Épenots, Pommard Rugiens, Pommard Clos-de-la-Commaraine, Volnay Caillerets, Volnay Santenots.

Good ($5 to $9): Beaune Teurons, Fixin Clos de la Perrière, Morey-St. Denis Clos des Lambrays, Nuits-St. Georges Les Vaucrains, Volnay Champans, Vosne-Romanée Les Suchots.

Shipper blends

Immediately below the commune-vineyard wines, in quality, are the commune blends, named for a commune alone, as, for example, *Pommard* or *Nuits-St. Georges*. The quality of these, of course, depends partly on the quality of wine in the commune generally and partly on the shipper who blends it. Lists of the better communes and shippers are given below.

In a still lesser category are burgundies labeled *Côte de Beaune* or *Côte de Nuits* (the two geographical halves of the Côte d'Or), quite often with the word *villages* attached to them. These are blends of wine from any of the communes in the district—but probably not the better communes. (*Côte de Beaune,* by the way, should not be confused with *Beaune,* a fine commune name.) Lastly, there are wines marked simply *Bourgogne* (Burgundy). These are the least impressive Burgundy wines, made from any vineyard throughout the entire region. Even so, be sure they bear the words *Appellation Bourgogne Contrôlée,* for there are many "burgundies" that lack even this measure of authenticity and, therefore, may not be burgundies at all.

In all of these lesser-priced wines, the shipper plays a crucial role. Even in the finest vineyards some growers have more wine-making skill and/or better holdings than do others, and the good shippers take advantage of these, knowing which wines to buy and

Those Confusing Burgundy Names

Not infrequently in Burgundy's Côte d'Or you will find the name of a famous vineyard turning up as part of the name of a less renowned vineyard or even of the commune itself. All it takes is a hyphen and a court decree. The reason for it is obvious: The lesser vineyard or commune hopes that some of the renown will rub off on it.

Thus, in 1847, the commune of Gevrey became Gevrey-Chambertin, presumably so that its wines might cash in on the illustrious reputation of its best-known vineyard, Chambertin. Eight other vineyards in Gevrey—all *grand crus* themselves—also appropriated the name with the result that we now have Chambertin-Clos de Beze, Chapelle-Chambertin, etc. Other hyphenated communes are: Aloxe-Corton (after the vineyard Corton), Chambolle-Musigny (after Musigny), Chassagne-Montrachet and Puligny-Montrachet (both after Montrachet, which straddles the communes), and Vosne-Romanée (after Romanée). Some of these communes produce excellent commune wines, but they should not be confused with wines from the famous vineyards included in their names.

how to blend them. The final prices may not always reflect these discrepancies, but CU's consultants are well aware of them and have, in consequence, evaluated the producers and shippers (*négociants*) very carefully in the lists below.

SOME RECOMMENDED RED BURGUNDY COMMUNE WINES

The following communes, graded into two categories by CU's consultants, are considered to offer the better wines at this level, particularly if the wine is from one of the recommended shippers listed below.

Very Good ($4 to $8): Aloxe-Corton, Beaune, Chambolle-Musigny, Gevrey-Chambertin, Nuits-St. Georges, Vosne-Romanée.

Good ($4 to $8): Auxey-Duresses, Chassagne-Montrachet, Fixin, Monthélie, Morey-St. Denis, Pernand-Vergelesses, Pommard, Santenay, Savigny-les-Beaune, Volnay.

SOME RECOMMENDED SHIPPERS OF RED BURGUNDY WINES

The following lists of shippers recommended by CU's consultants should be used as a general guide only, since it was based on a judgment of the overall quality of the shipper's wines. Your own selections could well be influenced by a wine merchant's recommendations or your own tasting.

Very Good: Bouchard Père & Fils, Joseph Drouhin, J. Faiveley, Henri Gouges, Jaboulet-Vercherre, Louis Jadot, Louis Latour, Jacques Prieur, A. Ropiteau-Mignon, Armand Rousseau & Fils.

Good: B & G, Bichot, Bouchard Ainé & Fils, L. J. Bruck, Calvet & Cie, Chanson Père & Fils, Cruse & Fils Frères, Domaine Grivelet, Jouvet, Lichine, Ligèr-Belair, Moillard Grivot, Mommessin, Morin, de Moucheron & Cie, Patriarche, Piat, Prosper Maufoux, Reine Pédauque, Sichel & Fils Frères.

Beaujolais

Beaujolais is typically a light-bodied, fruity wine, often described as having a pleasant freshness if drunk—as it should be, according to CU's consultants—before it is three years old, preferably within a year or even less. The Beaujolais district is at the south end of Burgundy, with different soil conditions from those of the Côte d'Or and with a different grape variety. Beaujolais is made from the gamay grape, which makes an inferior wine if grown in the Côte d'Or. (Conversely, the pinot noir grape of "true" burgundies produces disappointing wine in the soil of Beaujolais.)

The wines of Beaujolais are never great. To be good values, they should be (but are not always) reasonable in price. Very few beaujolais wines are estate-bottled, but the following hints may help you pick out a better blend.

Beaujolais Supérieur is usually preferable to just plain *Beaujolais,* but there is not a great deal of difference. *Beaujolais-Villages* is a definite step higher in quality. The finest beaujolais wines bear a commune name; these wines are required to meet much stricter standards. They are worth searching out, CU's consultants say, for you will almost certainly get a much better wine, and the added cost (about $1 more than plain beaujolais) may well be worth it.

SOME RECOMMENDED RED BEAUJOLAIS WINES

Following are the nine communes recognized as producing the better beaujolais wines, graded into two groups by CU's consultants. Since these will be shipper blends, refer to the list of recommended burgundy shippers (facing page) when you shop for these wines. In addition, the following shippers are noted particularly for beaujolais: Jacques Depagneux, Pasquier-Desvignes & Cie, Jean Thorin.

Very Good ($3 to $5): Brouilly, Côte-de-Brouilly, Fleurie, Moulin-a-Vent.

Good ($3 to $5): Chénas, Chiroubles, Juliénas, Morgon, St. Amour.

Red Rhône Valley wines

After beaujolais and the wines of Bordeaux and Burgundy, the French red wine most familiar to Americans is probably château-neuf-du-pape. It is in all likelihood the best-known wine of the Rhône region, although—in the opinion of CU's consultants—not the best in quality. That distinction, they feel, should be accorded the wine labeled *Côte Rôtie* ("roasted slope"). Made primarily from the syrah grape, it comes from the northernmost vineyards of the region, on a slope that faces south and takes the sun all summer. Côte rôtie has a more delicate flavor and a stronger bouquet than châteauneuf-du-pape, which is typically full-bodied and deep in color. Comparatively high in alcohol (12½ to 14 per cent or more), châteauneuf-du-pape is a blend of as many as thirteen types of grapes. Another full-bodied Rhône is hermitage, noted for its fragrant bouquet.

For good value among Rhône wines, CU's consultants recommend the relatively low-priced wines of Côtes-du-Rhône Gigondas and Crozes-Hermitage. The former (from a commune near Avignon) is a lesser châteauneuf-du-pape; the latter, a lesser hermitage.

SOME RECOMMENDED RED RHÔNE WINES

CU's consultants have listed, for each of six Rhône districts, estate- or monopole-named wines (with the shipper's name in parentheses) or a shipper's wine given simply under his own name. In addition to those listed, some of the large bordeaux shippers (page 35) and burgundy shippers (page 40) also offer Rhône wines under their own labels. They will usually be lower in price and somewhat lower in quality.

CÔTE RÔTIE

Very Good ($4.85 to $5.50): Chapoutier, Domaine Gerin, J. Vidal Fleury.

HERMITAGE

Very Good ($3.55 to $4.85): La Chapelle (Paul Jaboulet), Mure de la Sizeranne (Chapoutier), Rochefine (Jaboulet-Vercherre).

CHÂTEAUNEUF-DU-PAPE

Good ($3.75 to $5.50): Château Fortia (Baron Le Roy), Delas Frères, Domaine de Mont Redon (Plantin), La Bernadine (Chapoutier), Paul Jaboulet Ainé, Père Anselme, A. Rochette & Cie, Réserve des Ministres (Tytell).

CÔTES-DU-RHÔNE

Good ($2 to $2.40): Bichot, Delas Frères, A. de Luze & Fils, Jaboulet-Vercherre, Piat Père & Fils.

CÔTES-DU-RHÔNE GIGONDAS

Good ($3 to $3.65): A. Bessac, Chapoutier, Domaine des Pradets.

CROZES-HERMITAGE

Good ($2.80 to $3.20): Les Meysonniers, Chapoutier, Paul Jaboulet Aine, Salavert.

Good values in other French red wines

A number of other regions in France produce red wines that are pleasant, if not fine, wines. Because they are not well known, they may be (when available) good values. CU's consultants suggest the following as worth looking for: Bourgueil (also St. Nicolas-de-Bourgueil) and Chinon, both from the Touraine district of the Loire Valley; and Bandol, from the Provence region along the Mediterranean.

RED WINES OF ITALY

Although Italy is second only to France in quantity of table wine exported to this country, Italian wine, for most Americans, means a straw-covered bottle of chianti—low in price and undistinguished in quality. However, Italy produces a number of very good, even great, red wines (including some very fine chiantis), and many of these represent good value for the money. Italian red wines are generally less expensive than French red wines or some U.S. premium wines. Moreover, progress is being made in countering their tendency to vary from batch to batch—a curious tendency, in any case, since almost all of them are blends. The better Italian wines—and this means nearly all 'those exported to this country—now carry the words *Denominazione de Origine Controllata,* a government guarantee system instituted in 1963 and designed after the *Appellation Contrôlée* labeling in France. Since the system is still relatively new, it doesn't yet have the stature of the French, but you can certainly buy Italian wines with a great deal more confidence than in years past.

Many Italian wines are named after the place in which they originate, but the place can be a rather large district, as for chianti, or just a town, as for barolo. Other wines are known by the grape they are made from—barbera, for example. Once you know the type of Italian wine you want (and CU's consultants have limited their Recommendations to the leading six), the key to getting better wines is the producer's name on the bottle. In their Recommendations, CU's consultants list the better producers for each type of wine.

Real chianti, from Tuscany, is a very positive and full-flavored dry wine, ideal with hearty Italian dishes. The best chiantis, which will have been aged, are found in bordeaux-type bottles (see page 14). Such a chianti will almost always be superior to one in the straw-wrapped *fiasco,* CU's consultants note. But an even surer way of identifying the better chiantis is to look for one of the distinctive neck labels issued by a *consorzio* (local wine society). A black cockerel adorns the seal on *chianti classico* wines, from the district credited with originating chianti. A cherub is on the seal of chiantis made in a less narrowly delimited area of Tuscany, and there are a number of other seals that designate specially restricted areas producing the superior chiantis.

From near Verona in northeastern Italy come two wines with little of the sharpness of chianti. Bardolino and valpolicella are a deep ruby color, pleasantly fruity, and smooth. Valpolicella, with a delicate bouquet, is softer-tasting than bardolino.

Rivaling the best chiantis as the finest Italian table wine is barolo, in the opinion of CU's consultants. This is a pungent, full-bodied wine, deep red in color, from the Piedmont region in northwestern Italy. Barolo benefits from aging; older vintages are sometimes available—at a price. Two other good red wines of the Piedmont are named after grape varieties, grignolino and barbera (which is sometimes harsh, but can be very good). In addition, you may wish to try freisa (a light, fruity wine) and gattinara, though they are not so widely distributed here.

SOME RECOMMENDED ITALIAN RED WINES

Following are recommended producers of six major types of Italian red wines, graded into two categories by CU's consultants. The name of the producer will usually appear prominently on the label along with the name of the wine. Prices given are for the standard bottle, unless otherwise indicated. Star (★) indicates those wines also bottled in half-gallon and/or gallon sizes.

CHIANTI

Very Good ($2.25 to $4.35): Brolio Riserva, Frescobaldi, Machiavelli, Nozzole, Palazzo Al Bosco, Ruffino Riserva Ducale, Straccali, Villa Antinori.

Good ($2.95 to $3.75 for quart): Bertolli★, Brolio★, Frescobaldi★, Melini★, Ricasoli★, Ruffino★, Soderi★.

BAROLO

Very Good ($3 to $6.50): Borgogno, Calissano, Contratto, Francofredda, Marchesi di Barolo.

Good ($4 to $6.50): Bersano★, Cella, Marchesi Spinola.

BARBERA

Good ($2.50 to $3): Borgogno, Bersano★, Calissano, Cella, Contratto.

BARDOLINO and VALPOLICELLA

Good ($2.25 to $3.35): Antinori, Bertani★, Bolla★, Cantina Sociale, Folonari★, Frassine, Lamberti★, Montresor, Ricasoli, Ruffino★, Sartori.

GRIGNOLINO

Good ($2.50 to $3.05): Borgogno, Bersano★, Calissano, Cella.

RED WINES OF SPAIN

The table wines of Spain are, in many cases, extremely variable in quality and characteristics, but they are generally low priced. Thus, when they are good, and some can be very good, they are usually very good buys.

The red wines of the Rioja district, in northeastern Spain, are unquestionably the finest red table wines of the country. These wines are similar in some ways to bordeaux reds, but have a distinguishable flavor of their own. A quality indication to look for is a label reading *Garantía de Origen.* Riojas designated *Reserva* have been aged longer. CU's consultants believe that the brands listed below offer exceptional value for the money.

(The name "sangría" is frequently associated with Spanish wines, but sangría is not a particular kind of wine. It is a traditional Spanish wine-and-fruit punch made, typically, with oranges and lemons, often with brandy and/or soda added. Ready-to-pour versions are widely sold but, though a refreshing drink, cannot be considered "table wine" in the usual sense.)

SOME RECOMMENDED SPANISH RED WINES

Listed below are producers of the better Spanish red wines (most are riojas), graded into two groups by CU's consultants. Prices are shown for a standard bottle. Any that are shipped in half-gallon and/or gallon sizes are indicated by a star (★).

Very Good (About $3): Marqués de Murrieta, Marqués de Riscal, Miguel Torres Gran Reserva Coronas, Paternina Gran Reserva.

Good ($1.70 to $3): Alella Marfil, C.V.N.E. Imperial, Juan Hernandez★, La Rioja Alta Vina Ardanza, Miguel Torres Coronas, Paternina Banda Azul, Rene Barbier Tinto, Rioja Ederra, Siglo, Vina Pomal, Vizconde de Ayala.

RED WINES OF THE UNITED STATES

Most of the American table wine marketed in the United States is produced in California. Only about 15 per cent comes from the eastern states (primarily New York); the eastern red wines are described on page 52.

California red wines

Much of California's table-wine production is ordinary in quality, but among the small proportion of superior products are some that stand up very well to all but the finest imported wines. Most of the quality table wines come from northern California, around the San Francisco Bay area. Grapes are grown throughout the state, but in the more southerly regions it is too hot for the best wine-grape varieties to grow properly. In all areas of California the climate is fairly equable so that, except for the very finest wines, vintage years are usually not considered very important.

The best California wines are found among the so-called *varietal* wines. By law, a wine may be named after a grape variety—say, cabernet sauvignon—provided that variety accounts for at least 51 per cent of the grapes used in the vatting.

Incidentally, the cabernet sauvignon grape is the variety identified with the French bordeaux (clarets). It is not necessarily found in a "California claret," however, for the latter, a *generic* wine, is merely a blend named, but often only very loosely patterned, after a foreign original. Some California wineries eschew recognition of their product by either grape variety or borrowed name, preferring instead to use a *proprietary* brand name or trademark. Generic and proprietary wines are discussed later.

Varietal wines

Cabernet sauvignon (or cabernet) comes from what is probably California's most successful red-wine grape—successful not only in terms of the quality of the wines made from it but also in terms of the recent prices that these wines command. The best cabernet sauvignons are generally considered California's, and America's, finest red wines. Slightly fuller in body than the French red wines of Bordeaux, they have a rich red color and the distinctive cabernet aroma. When the wine is comparatively young, the flavor may be fruity but slightly bitter; after sufficient aging, good examples develop a subtle, complex, and herblike flavor. Properly stored, California cabernets will generally continue to improve in the bottle for many years; typically, they are at their best between five and twelve years old. Most California producers of fine varietals date

If You Visit California

There are in California certain small vineyards whose production is so limited that the wines rarely leave the vineyard, much less the state. These vineyards usually specialize in a few varietals, reds and/or whites. Their wines are so exceptional that their production is often committed to buyers in advance, but sometimes they can be found in California stores or bought on a visit to the vineyard itself. With such limited production, it is no surprise that their prices are higher than those for the standard varietals. CU's consultants suggest you keep an eye out for wines from the following vineyards: Bernard Fetzer, Chalone, Chappellet, David Bruce, Freemark Abbey, Hanzell, Llords & Elwood, Mayacamas, Ridge, Souverain, Stony Hill.

their wines, because these finer wines do vary somewhat in quality with each vintage. For the consumer who wants to store his wine, the year label tells him the age of the bottle. Since California law requires that all the wine in a bottle labeled with a year be from that vintage, those producers who do not year-label can standardize their wines by blending in some produced in other years. Each way has its advantages, and CU's consultants suggest you try both year-labeled and undated varietals.

In many cases, cabernet sauvignon is the producer's highest-priced wine—as the prices of the recommended wines would indicate. In addition, CU's consultants think the following special (and higher-priced) cabernet bottlings should be excellent—higher in quality than any of those listed below: Beaulieu Vineyard Private Reserve ($5.55), Inglenook Cabernet Sauvignon (Cask) ($5.95), and Louis Martini Cabernet Sauvignon Special Selection ($5.30). (For other special cabernets, see our list of small producers, box just above.) These are all limited in distribution. So is Martin Ray, which sells for exceptional prices ranging from $15 to $20, but our consultants have found the wine unexceptional. As surprising as these prices seem, the trend indicates even higher prices for the finest California wines in the future.

A second varietal, pinot noir, comes from the other "noble" red-wine grape of California. It produces a ruby-colored wine with a fine bouquet and a flavor that has been described as pepperminty. California pinot noirs tend to be lighter-bodied than the wine made from this grape in Burgundy.

Gamay and gamay beaujolais are also ruby-colored wines, but lighter-bodied than the pinot noir. These gamay varieties differ slightly, but both are similar to the grape of the original beaujolais. As in France, the wine is never great but usually good and pleasantly fruity.

Zinfandel is named for California's own special grape variety, grown almost nowhere else but thriving there for more than a century. Today this grape is the state's most productive and most widely grown variety. Consequently, zinfandel wines are usually inexpensive. They are pleasant and medium-bodied and have a spicy fruitiness that reminds some people of raspberries.

Three other red varietals should be mentioned, though their production is far more limited than the types above. Barbera, one of the famous grapes of Italy's Piedmont, is made into a full, fruity California varietal by several producers; CU's consultants recommend those from Louis Martini and Sebastiani, priced at about $2.50. Charbono, another Italian grape, is not widely grown but has become something of a house specialty at the Inglenook vineyards. Their charbono varietal is a fine wine, according to our consultants, and the price reflects its premium quality, about $3.15. Petite sirah, usually used as a blending grape, is now seen as a varietal, priced at about $3. Mirassou and Concannon are major producers.

SOME RECOMMENDED CALIFORNIA RED VARIETAL WINES

Following are lists of producers of the four major red varietals, graded into three groups by CU's consultants. Though some of the producers make a "special" or "reserve" wine, the wines listed here are their standard varietals.

CABERNET SAUVIGNON

Very Good ($2.50 to $4.20): Beaulieu, Buena Vista, Christian Brothers, Inglenook, Charles Krug, Louis Martini, Mirassou, Robert Mondavi.

Good ($2.50 to $4.20): Almadén, Beringer, Cresta Blanca, Korbel, Paul Masson.

PINOT NOIR

Very Good ($2.50 to $4.50): Beaulieu, Heitz, Inglenook, Charles Krug, Louis Martini, Robert Mondavi.

Good ($2.50 to $4): Almadén, Christian Brothers, Korbel, Paul Masson, Sebastiani, Wente.

GAMAY (or GAMAY BEAUJOLAIS)

Good ($2.65 to $2.80): Almadén, Charles Krug, Paul Masson, Mirassou, Wente.

ZINFANDEL

Good ($2.15 to $2.70): Inglenook, Louis Martini, Mirassou, Wente.

Fair ($2.15 to $2.70): Almadén, Beringer, Buena Vista, Christian Brothers, Villa Armando.

Generic wines

California's generic wines are its *vins ordinaires*. Generics use the names of well-known European wines (burgundy, for example), but they are actually blends of any grape wines that the producer wishes to use to achieve the taste he is aiming at. For economic reasons, it is not likely that much wine of renowned grape varieties will be used in a generic blend, for most varietal vines do not produce an abundant yield, and their grapes are in short supply. The generics are lower in price than the varietals, of course, and are often produced in larger-than-fifth bottles. They are not, for the most part, year-labeled. Since they are blended to a specific taste, they will be found uniform from bottle to bottle. If you find one you like, you can be sure of what you're getting the next time—a good recipe for an everyday wine, according to our consultants. Their choices are shown below.

SOME RECOMMENDED CALIFORNIA RED GENERIC WINES

Following are lists of producers of the three major red generic wines, selected by CU's consultants. Since many of these are produced in larger sizes, price ranges are given for half-gallons and gallons as well. Those marked with a star (★) come in larger sizes, in half-gallons and/or gallons.

CLARET

Good ($1.60 to $2; half-gallon, $3.20 to $4.25; gallon, $5.30 to $7.85): Almadén Mountain Red★, Christian Brothers★, Cresta Blanca★.

BURGUNDY

Good ($1.15 to $2.10; half-gallon, $2.25 to $4.25; gallon, $3.80 to $7.85): Beaulieu, CK-Mondavi★, Fior di California Burgundy Scelto★, Gallo Hearty Burgundy★, Guild★, Louis Martini Mountain Red★, Paul Masson★.

CHIANTI

Good ($1.15 to $1.40; half-gallon, $2.35 to $2.90; gallon, $4 to $4.90): CK-Mondavi★, Gallo★, Italian Swiss Colony★, Romano Cucamonga★.

Proprietary wines

Instead of labeling their blends with generic names, some producers make up their own names, to set the wines apart. These are called "proprietary" wines, since the name belongs only to the one producer. Baroque, a burgundy-type wine, and Rubion, a claret type, both made by Paul Masson, are examples of such wines. Since proprietary wines are blended to an individual producer's taste, there is little comparison to be made between them, and our consultants did not make recommendations in this group. Occasionally, producers will give a proprietary name to varietals or generics, in addition to the name of the varietal or the generic, but they are normally better known by the latter. Beaulieu's pinot noir, which they also call Beaumont, is an example.

New York and Ohio red wines

The wines of the Finger Lakes district of New York and of Ohio's Lake Erie shore are produced mainly from grape varieties developed from native vines, the *vitis labrusca*. These wines, particularly the reds, tend to differ greatly from the European wines for which they are often named, primarily because of the strong grapey flavor carried by the labrusca grape. CU's consultants suggest, therefore, that you do not try to match these wines to their European prototypes but instead judge them on their own.

For years only generic wines were made by the producers in New York and Ohio—burgundies, for example—but recently some adventurous vineyard owners have been working with hybrid vines— crosses between the European vinifera and the American labrusca— to produce new strains with greater quality and the necessary hardiness. Now there are varietals as well from this area.

SOME SUGGESTED
NEW YORK STATE RED WINES

Among the hybrids and varietals, our consultants suggest looking for the following: Benmarl Vineyards Rouge Domaine (a hybrid varietal), Boordy Vineyards red (a blend of hybrids), Bully Hill red (a blend of hybrids), Great Western's Baco Noir and Chelois (two hybrid varietals), High Tor Rockland Red (a blend of hybrids), and Widmer's Isabella (a native varietal). Prices range from $1.90 to $3.75. Among the generics suggested are clarets by Hudson Valley, Taylor, and Widmer, and burgundies by Gold Seal, Great Western, Hudson Valley, Taylor, and Widmer. Prices range from $1.80 to $2.25.

RED WINES FROM OTHER COUNTRIES

Of the scores of other countries that produce table wines, a great many have some representation, however sparse, among the thousands of imported wines available in the United States. France, Italy, Spain, and Germany account for more than 90 per cent of table-wine imports. The countries included in the remaining 8 or 9 per cent send us products that, being little known, are often com-

paratively low in price. Whether or not they are also low in quality
is a matter for experimentation. If you are moderately adventurous,
you might discover some fine values by trying these "unknown"
wines. Here are some reds CU's consultants suggest you look for,
with brands (in most cases) and approximate prices per fifth.

From *Argentina,* a mellow red (San Felipe Tinto, $2.50). From
Australia, a burgundy (B. Seppelt & Sons, $2.70). From *Chile,* a
cabernet sauvignon (Concha y Toro, $2) and a pinot noir (Un-
durraga, $2). From *Cyprus,* a dry red called Keo Othello ($2).
From *Greece,* a light red called Pendeli (Cambas, $2). From
Hungary, a dark, heavy wine called Egri Bikavér ($2.85). From
Israel, a cabernet sauvignon (C.W.G., $2.35). From *Portugal,* a
rather coarse red called Dão (Gran Vasco, $2.55). From *Switzer-
land,* a perfumed gamay called Dôle de Sion (Châtenay, $3.50).
From *Yugoslavia,* reds called Tlavac ($2) and Prokupac (Navip,
$1.80).

Chapter 4

ROSÉ WINES

Though red wines cannot be made from white grapes, white wines can be—and often are—made from red grapes. Remove the skins from the vat right after pressing, and you have white wine (see page 57). Let them remain for a short time—one to three days— and you have pink wine: *vin rosé.* (Some inexpensive rosé wines are a mixture of red and white wines, but they are usually of inferior quality.)

Rosés are lighter-bodied than red wines but often have some of the characteristic red-wine tartness. Customarily they are served chilled. Although their popularity seems to be increasing steadily in the United States, they are not numbered by connoisseurs among the finer kinds of wines. Still, good rosés are thoroughly pleasant and refreshing, particularly with a summer luncheon.

IMPORTED ROSÉ WINES

The original rosés were produced in the town of Tavel, France. Tavel rosés are crisp and dry, with a faint tendency toward harshness. Most imported rosés are very dry, except for the slightly sweet rosés from Anjou (some are made in dry, semisweet, and sweet versions) and Lancers, the well-known Portuguese rosé, which is not only slightly sweet but, relatively speaking, more than slightly expensive. The other Portuguese rosés listed below are light, dry wines. Many of these are relatively new wines for the United States, following on the success of earlier Portuguese rosés, such as Mateus, and they are of comparable quality and still relatively inexpensive. Some of the Italian rosés are very pleasant. They may be labeled *chiaretto,* a word meaning light in color. Though CU's consultants made no specific recommendations of Italian rosés, they suggest you look for those from Lake Garda.

SOME RECOMMENDED FRENCH ROSÉ WINES

For each of four districts of France, CU's consultants have selected rosés to recommend. The wines are listed by district and graded into two quality groups. The name given (either a brand name or the name of the shipper) will appear clearly on the bottle along with the district designation.

TAVEL (Rhône)

Very Good ($3.25 to $4): Chapoutier & Cie, Château d'Aqueria, Paul Jaboulet, Sichel & Fils Frères.

ANJOU (Loire)

Good ($2 to $2.60): Ackerman-Lawrence, Amourosé, E. Blanchard & Fils, Gonnet Rosé de Sancerre, Nectarosé, Remy-Pannier, Sichel & Fils Frères, Tytell.

BURGUNDY

Good ($3.20): Rosé de Marsannay (Clair Dau).

PROVENCE

Good ($2.25 to $4): Château de Selle, Château des Vannières, Château Ste. Roseline, Domaine de Boisseaux-Rosé de Bandol, Domaine de Moulières, Moulin des Costes.

SOME RECOMMENDED PORTUGUESE ROSÉ WINES

The following Portuguese rosés have been selected by CU's consultants and are listed either under a brand name or the shipper's name.

Good ($1.60 to $2.90): Alianca, Bravera, Castelo Real, Costa Do Sol, Dom Brazilio, Empress, Fonseca, Isabel, Lagosta, Mateus, Pombal, Trovador, Vinya.

ROSÉ WINES OF THE UNITED STATES

California rosé is rather dry and light-bodied and very pleasant to drink; it is not markedly dissimilar to European rosé. CU's consultants consider California rosé made primarily from either grenache or gamay grapes to have more character and to be of higher quality than those made from a variety of grapes.

New York State and Ohio rosés are somewhat more full-bodied than the California rosés. They have a rich flavor and bouquet and although they bear little resemblance to the rosés of Europe, they are agreeable wines in their own right.

SOME RECOMMENDED
CALIFORNIA ROSÉ WINES

The following rosés selected by CU's consultants are made from one or more of the good grape varieties (cabernet, gamay, or grenache). Star (★) indicates those available in half-gallons and/or gallons.

Good ($1.70 to $2.45): Almadén★, Beaulieu, Buena Vista, Christian Brothers, Inglenook★, Louis Martini★, Paul Masson★, Robert Mondavi, Wente.

SOME SUGGESTED
NEW YORK STATE AND OHIO ROSÉ WINES

The following rosés suggested by our consultants are all from New York, except Meier's, and are generics unless otherwise indicated. They range from $1.70 to $2.15. Star (★) indicates wines that come in larger sizes: Gold Seal "Catawba Pink"★ (varietal), Great Western's "Isabella Rose" (varietal), Meier's, Taylor's, Widmer's "Lake Roselle"★.

Chapter 5

WHITE WINES

White table wines range in color from palest straw to brownish gold. They are more delicate than red wines, for they contain less tannin, or tannic acid, which comes from the skin of the grape and adds to the flavor, body, and longevity of a wine. Whether bone dry or syrupy sweet or somewhere in between, white table wines are usually served chilled.

WHITE WINES OF FRANCE

Bordeaux and Burgundy are noted not only for their red wines but for their white wines as well. There are also many esteemed white wines from Alsace, the Loire Valley, and the Côtes du Rhône.

White bordeaux

The principal white wines of Bordeaux are those of Graves, which are dry, and those of Sauternes, which are sweet. Sauternes are still considered table wines rather than dessert wines even though today many more people serve them at the end of the meal than with the pâté or fish course, as they used to. Somewhat less sweet than sauternes and constituting a sort of subgroup within them are the wines of Barsac, a subdistrict within Sauternes.

While most of the graves available here are district wines, there are some outstanding château-bottlings, which our consultants describe as being elegant wines of character and finesse. They are listed on page 59.

True sauternes is simply not what many Americans have in mind when they think of "sauterne." Often spelled here without the final "s," the domestic version of this great wine is almost always dry and not at all memorable. Sauternes itself is a few miles south of Graves, and its grapes are the same as those that are responsible for the dry, white Graves wines. But the Sauternes grapes are picked late, just before the first frosts, at the point when their overripeness has resulted in the development of botrytis, a disease also called *le pourriture noble* (the noble rot). It attacks the grape, cracks the skin, and permits air and sun to remove part of the water content. The result is a rich pulp, heavy with sugar which quickly ferments to 14 per cent alcohol and still leaves unfermented sugar in the wine. This is the reason for the sweetness (a quality the French call *liquoreux*) of the great sauternes and barsacs.

Among the château-bottled sauternes is what is probably the most famous of all white wines, that of Château d'Yquem, which the French call *hors classe,* or "beyond compare." Other fine château-bottled sauternes, if not always quite so outstanding as d'Yquem, are always less expensive. If these wines appeal to you, our consultants consider them very good buys for wines of this caliber (see list at top of facing page).

Other dry white bordeaux come from Blaye, Bourg, Entre-Deux-Mers; other sweet white bordeaux come from Cérons and Premières Côtes de Bordeaux. Within the latter district the most notable communes are Loupiac and Ste. Croix-du-Mont. Most of these wines are relatively low-priced, and, with a bit of searching, you may find among them some that you'll consider exceptionally good values. They will be district or commune blends.

The shippers of white bordeaux wines are the same as those who ship red bordeaux (see list of recommended shippers, page 35).

SOME RECOMMENDED
WHITE BORDEAUX CHÂTEAUX WINES

Following are châteaux from the two Bordeaux districts, Sauternes and Graves, graded by CU's consultants into three groups.

SAUTERNES
Excellent ($3.50 to $5): Ch. Climens, Ch. Coutet, Ch. Filhot, Ch. Guiraud, Ch. Lafaurie-Peyraguey, Ch. LaTour Blanche, Ch. de Rayne-Vigneau, Ch. Rieussec, Ch. Suduiraut.

GRAVES
Outstanding ($7 to $15): Domaine de Chevalier, Ch. Haut-Brion Blanc.

Excellent ($4 to $5): Ch. Couhins, Ch. Laville-Haut Brion.

Very Good ($4 to $5): Ch. Bouscaut, Ch. Carbonnieux, Ch. La Tour Martillac, Ch. Olivier.

White burgundies

The more important white wines of Burgundy come from the districts of the Côte d'Or, Chablis, and the Maconnais. All are made from the chardonnay grape, and all are (or should be) extremely dry—and there the similiarities end, for they are all wines of distinctive character.

Aside from a small quantity produced in the communes of Aloxe-Corton and Vougeot, the great Côte d'Or white wines come from Meursault, Chassagne-Montrachet, and Puligny-Montrachet. The last two communes share between them the great vineyard of Montrachet itself, whose twenty acres produce what is reputed to be the greatest dry white wine in the world. Certainly it is the most expensive, with recent vintages commanding up to $30 and more for a bottle. Montrachet is also *hors classe.*

Côte d'Or whites are rather full-bodied and are longer-lived than most other white wines, although they are thoroughly enjoyable when they are young, too. Estate-bottled wines are available from the great vineyards (see list on next page). Shippers' commune blends will almost certainly be much less expensive than the estate-bottled wines.

The green-tinged, yellowish wines of Chablis, drunk while they are young, have a crisp, clean tang that the many non-French "chablis" seldom even approximate. There are, generally speaking, four classes of French chablis. Of the estate-bottled chablis those that are officially proclaimed *grand cru* carry the name of one of the seven great vineyards from which they come. A *premier cru* chablis carries the name of its vineyard (any one of twenty-two) plus the name of the commune in which the vineyard is located. Also available, as shipper blends, are *chablis* and *petit chablis*. Chablis—the name unqualified—designates the largest class of this wine: good but not outstanding. In fourth—and bottom—position is petit chablis, but this can on occasion be a pleasant surprise particularly in a good year for the area.

The best wine of the Maconnais district is pouilly-fuissé, a sharp, brisk wine very popular in this country. It is most attractive in its second and third years. On the labels of the best pouilly-fuissé you will find the name of the responsible vineyard. Shipper blends of pouilly-fuissé are readily available, but, due to its popularity, are not inexpensive.

SOME RECOMMENDED WHITE BURGUNDY WINES

Following are estate-bottled or commune blends selected by CU's consultants from the two major Burgundy areas and graded into three quality groups.

CÔTE D'OR

Outstanding (estate-bottled) ($7 to $15): Bâtard-Montrachet, Bienvenue-Bâtard-Montrachet, Chevalier-Montrachet, Corton-Charlemagne, Musigny-Blanc.

Excellent (estate-bottled) ($6 to $8.50): Clos Blanc de Vougeot, Meursault-Genevrières, Meursault-Goutte d'Or, Meursault-Les Perrières, Puligny-Montrachet (Les Combettes), Puligny-Montrachet (Les Pucelles).

Very Good (commune blends) ($4 to $6): Chassagne-Montrachet, Meursault, Puligny-Montrachet.

CHABLIS

Outstanding (grand crus) ($5 to $6.50): Bourgros, Blanchots, Les Clos, Grenouilles, Les Preuses, Valmur, Vaudésir.

Excellent (premier crus) ($4 to $6): Les Forêts, Fourchaume, Montmain, Montée de Tonnerre, La Moutonne, Vaillon.

SOME RECOMMENDED
SHIPPERS OF WHITE BURGUNDIES

In general, follow the recommendations given by CU's consultants for the shippers of red burgundies (page 40). They recommend the following especially for white burgundies: Joseph Drouhin, Louis Jadot, Louis Latour, J. Moreau, Albert Pic.

Alsatian white wines

In northeast France, running pretty well the length of the old province of Alsace, is a narrow strip of land on which vineyards have been cultivated since Roman times.

Today, like the varietal wines of California, Alsatian wines are named for the grape variety from which they are produced rather than for their place of origin. Since the varieties grown on the Alsatian side of the Rhine are the same as the varieties grown on the German side, there are clear family resemblances between Alsatian and German rhine wines (see page 63). For one thing, in both areas all the notable wines are white. The wines of Alsace have their own character, however; they are fresh, fragrant, and rather full-flavored, and they are usually drunk young.

The finest Alsatian wines are riesling (dry, clean, fresh) and gewürztraminer. Following them are traminer (*gewürz* means spicy—gewürztraminer is fuller, richer, sweeter than traminer) and sylvaner (fruity, medium-bodied). An Alsatian wine that does not have a varietal name is likely to be inferior—and also lower in price. It may be labeled *Edelzwicker* (a better blend of "noble" grapes) or simply *Zwicker* (a lesser blend of any grapes). In addition to the varietal name, the labels of some of the better Alsatian wines provide the name of the commune (and, on rare occasions, the vineyard) as well as the shipper.

SOME RECOMMENDED
SHIPPERS OF ALSATIAN WHITE WINES

The following shippers are recommended by CU's consultants. All ship the four major Alsation varietals. Prices for these shippers' blends range from $2 to $4.50.

Good: E. Boeckel, Château de Mittelwihr, Domaine Willm, Domaines Dopff, Dopff & Irion, F. E. Hugel & Fils, Jerome Lorentz Fils, Sichel & Fils Frères, F. E. Trimbach.

Loire Valley white wines

The Loire Valley produces a number of pleasant, if never great, white wines, all with a touch of sweetness and a more or less flowery bouquet. The ones most popular in the United States are vouvray (either still or semisparkling), muscadet, sancerre, and pouilly-fumé (not to be confused with Burgundy's unrelated pouilly-fuissé). Particularly interesting in the opinion of CU's consultants are the Ladoucette pouilly-fumé (see list below) and two vouvrays, Château de Montcontour and Monmousseau. The two large overall districts in the Loire are Anjou and Touraine—wines so labeled will be lesser blends. In general, the Loire wines are best drunk when they are young.

SOME RECOMMENDED LOIRE VALLEY WHITE WINES

For each of the four good Loire Valley white wines, CU's consultants recommend producers whose names will be found on the label along with the name of the wine. They are graded into two groups.

MUSCADET

Good ($2 to $4.50): Ackerman-Lawrence, Château de la Bidere, Cuvée des Aigles, Domaine de Livernière.

POUILLY-FUMÉ

Very Good ($4.50): Ladoucette "Château du Nozet."

Good ($2.75): Ackerman-Lawrence Pouilly-Blanc Fumé.

SANCERRE

Good ($2 to $4.50): Ackerman-Lawrence, Château de Sancerre, Clos de la Perrière.

VOUVRAY

Very Good ($2 to $4.50): Château Montcontour, J. M. Monmousseau.

Good ($3.25): Remy-Pannier.

Côtes du Rhône white wines

White wines from the Rhône Valley do not have the stature of the reds. Among the best, say CU's consultants, are white hermitage, which is dry, light, and fragrant (they suggest specifically Chapoutier's Chante-Alouette, P. Jaboulet's La Chapelle, or those from Delas Frères and J. Vidal Fleury), and the soft, full-bodied châteauneuf-du-pape (they suggest Chapoutier's La Bernadine Blanc or Plantin's Domaine de Mont Redon).

WHITE WINES OF GERMANY

There is no German red wine of any importance, but some of the German whites are among the world's greatest. The two principal types, both produced mainly from riesling grapes, are rhine and moselle, named for the two river valleys in western Germany. The moselles are light and flowery, bottled in tall, slender *green* "flutes" (page 14), which hold 23-24 fluid ounces. The rhines are heavier and, usually, sweeter, bottled in *brown* glass. Both are still wines, though when young they are sometimes *spritzig,* as the Germans say, meaning they have a tingle on the tongue.

The good rhine wines come generally from three districts: Rheingau, Rheinhessen, and Rheinpfalz. There are, too, some good wines from the Nahe district (the Nahe is a small tributary of the Rhine), which are usually classified with the rhines. The moselles come, officially, from the area known as Moselle-Saar-Ruwer, the Saar and the Ruwer being tributaries of the Moselle. Most of the better moselles come from the Moselle itself, some from the Saar, and a few from the Ruwer, a much smaller district.

As a general principle, in Germany as in France, the more specific the geographic area, the finer the wine. Thus, the widely known liebfraumilch, which may be a blend of wines from any part of the Rhine, can be very poor or reasonably decent, depending on the shipper. The term means Milk of the Beloved Lady, and the wine is usually a soft, full-bodied, somewhat sweet blend. You will find it at a wide range of prices; the best of it is never very expensive and can be quite pleasant. Its moselle counterpart is moselblümchen. You would do well to rely on the shipper in making your choice, and CU's consultants have given a list of recommended shippers to look for (see pages 66-67).

Higher up on the quality scale are shippers' blends that take their name from the villages where the wines were produced. Erbach, Hattenheim, Hochheim, Johannisberg, Nierstein, Raudenthal, Rudesheim, and Steinberg are some of the Rhine villages with superb reputations. Bernkastel, Piesport, Urzig, Wehlen, and Zeltingen are some of the villages and districts where the good moselles originate. Even finer than these village wines would be those labeled also with a particular vineyard in the village, as for example *Niersteiner Rehbach.* (Nierstein is the village, Neirsteiner the wine, and Rehbach the vineyard.)

The labeling of fine wines in Germany has always been a formidable exercise in precision and conformity, but for the beginning label-reader it can seem more like hieroglyphics than a comprehensible language. In 1971 a new series of regulations was imposed on German wine producers designed to simplify their labels. Wines produced under the new regulations will begin to be seen in 1972, but the full effect of the laws will not be felt for another year or two. The basic change—and an important one for American consumers—was to establish three quality levels of German wine and require that the labels carry these designations: table wine *(Deutscher Tafelwein),* quality wine from selected regions *(Qualitätswein bestimmter Anbaugebiete),* and quality wine of distinction *(Qualitätswein mit Prädikat).* It is likely that only wines from the two higher levels will be seen in the United States.

Until these terms are in common use—and even after—you should know these additional marks of quality: *Kabinett* (has varied somewhat from producer to producer but will now be standardized to mean high-quality wine from fully matured grapes, without added sugar); *V.D.N.V.* (initials of the wine growers' association, showing that the wine adheres to certain strict standards); *spätlese,*

auslese, beerenauslese, and *trockenbeerenauslese* (four increasingly
fine degrees of specially picked grapes—the terms mean "late picking," "selected picking," "berry-selected picking," and "raisined
berry-selected picking"). The terms gradually being discarded—but
which you may still see for a while—are: *naturwein* or *natur* (indicating the wine was made without added sugar); *feine* or *feinste*
("fine" or "finest," which had no legal standing); and *fass* or *fuder*
(with a number, indicating "Cask #").

The finest of the German wines are estate-bottled, now indicated
by the words *Original-Abfüllung* on the label (sometimes abbreviated to *Orig.-Abfg.* or *O/A*). *Kellerabfüllung* is a less common but
equivalent term. Under the new laws these terms will give way to
Erzeugerabfüllung (bottled by the producer) and *aus eigenem
Lesegut* (from his own grapes).

In each of the major wine areas—the Rhine and the Moselle—
there is one wine whose fame has outstripped all others, with a
corresponding inflation in its price. Though the wines are outstanding, the high price is far more the result of scarcity than of unusual
superiority, in the opinion of CU's consultants.

From the Rhine there is Schloss Johannisberger, Fürst von
Metternich. It is perhaps the best-known—and most expensive—
of the fine German wines. Johannisberg is a village, the Schloss
(castle) Johannisberg is the dominant vineyard in the village, and
the estate owners are the descendants of Prince von Metternich,
of historic fame. The wine is graded with singular meticulousness
with seven quality levels shown by colors of the seal over the cork
and bottle neck. The highest level, a gold-sealed Kabinett wine, is
rare; a trockenbeerenauslese may well sell for as much as $90 a
bottle.

The outstanding estate-bottled moselle is Bernkasteler Doctor. The
town is Bernkastel and the vineyard is Doctor, now under three
owners, each of which produces wine of the highest (and more or
less equal) quality, in the opinion of CU's consultants. However,
this wine is always high-priced, for even its most abundant vintages
are inadequate for the world's demand.

SOME RECOMMENDED ESTATE-BOTTLED RHINE WINES

The following selections by CU's consultants are graded into three categories.

Excellent ($3.50 to $7): Schloss Johannisberger, Fürst von Metternich; Schloss Vollrads, Graf Matuschka-Greiffenclau; Steinberger, Staatsweingut.

Very Good ($3.50 to $6): Erbacher Markobrunn, Rauenthaler Baiken.

Good ($3.50 to $6): Deidesheimer Hohenmorgen, Forster Jesuitengarten, Hallgartener Schönhell, Hattenheimer Wisselbrunnen, Hochheimer Domdechaney, Niersteiner Rehbach, Oppenheimer Kreuz, Rüdesheimer Berg Rottland, Schloss Böckelheimer.

SOME RECOMMENDED ESTATE-BOTTLED MOSELLE WINES

The following selections by CU's consultants are graded into two categories.

Excellent ($10 to $16): Bernkasteler Doctor, Deinhard; Bernkasteler Doctor und Bratenhöfchen, J. Lauerburg; Bernkasteler Doctor und Graben, Dr. H. Thanisch.

Very Good ($4 to $6): Bernkasteler Lay, Brauneberger Juffer, Erdener Treppchen, Graacher Himmelreich, Maximin Grünhauser (Ruwer), Piesporter Goldtröpchen, Scharzhofberger (Saar), Ürziger Würzgarten, Wehlener Sonnenuhr.

SOME RECOMMENDED SHIPPERS OF GERMAN WINES

The following shippers (in some cases the shippers are producers as well) recommended by our consultants are graded into two groups. In general, the "outstanding" shippers are smaller and more specialized; the "very good" ones tend to be larger and often produce their own branded blends of liebfraumilch and moselblümchen.

Outstanding: Egon-Müller, Eltz, von Kesselstatt, Lauerburg, Matuschka, von Metternich, J. J. Prüm, S. A. Prüm, von Schönborn, von Schorlemer, von Schubert, Dr. H. Thanisch.

Very Good: Anheuser & Fehrs, Basserman Jordan, Deinhard, Guntrum, Hallgarten, Julius Kayser, Leonard Kreusch, Langenbach, Richard Langguth, H. von Mumm, Franz Karl Schmitt, Scholl & Hillebrand, H. Sichel Sohne, A. Steigenberger, Valckenberg, Franz Weber.

WHITE WINES OF ITALY

The Italian white wines exported to the United States are pleasant, light, relatively inexpensive, and deservedly popular. Nearly all are blends produced, in many cases, by the same firms known for their red wines.

A widely appreciated Italian white table wine is the dry, very smooth soave from Verona. Another is orvieto, from Umbria. Orvieto is traditionally a semisweet *(abboccato)* wine, delicate and delightful, but it is also available as a dry *(secco)* wine, also most agreeable.

At Montefiascone in Latium is produced a wine with the odd— and famous—name of est! est!! est!!! It, too, comes in both dry and sweet versions. Another wine from Latium is the dry, light-bodied frascati, one of the most frequently encountered white wines in and around Rome.

Less well known than any of the above wines but quite pleasant all the same is verdicchio dei castelli di jesi, often labeled just *verdicchio* (the name of the grape), a dry, refreshing wine from the Marches province, in east central Italy. Farther south, from Campania, the capital of which is Naples, come both lacrima christi, soft and fairly dry, and falerno, called by the ancient Romans falernum, semidry and medium-bodied. Neither of these is easy to come by. Of the Sicilian wines, two worth trying are corvo, a dry white (hard to find), and segesta, coarse but quite drinkable.

SOME RECOMMENDED
ITALIAN WHITE WINES

Following are producers of five major types of Italian white wines recommended by CU's consultants. The name of the producer, as well as the name of the wine, will appear prominently on the label.

SOAVE

Good ($2 to $3.25): Bertani, Bolla, Folonari, Ricasoli.

ORVIETO

Good ($2.15 to $3.15): Luigi Bigi, Melini, Petrurbani, Ruffino, Conte Vaselli.

EST! EST!! EST!!!

Good ($2.95): Antinori.

FRASCATI

Good ($2.45 to $3): Vini Fontana Candida, Fratelli Cella.

VERDICCHIO

Good ($2.70 to $3.15): Fazi-Battaglia, Aurora.

WHITE WINES OF CALIFORNIA

As it does for red wines, California produces whites in three categories—varietals, generics, and proprietary brands. (See the section on California reds [pages 46-51] for an explanation of these terms.) The varietals are normally of higher quality than the generics and, of course, cost somewhat more. The proprietary brands offer interesting variations that may appeal to individual tastes. Their cost falls roughly between the varietals and the generics.

Varietal white wines

Sauvignon blanc and semillon may be dry, semisweet, or sweet—never quite so dry as a bordeaux graves or so sweet as a bordeaux sauternes, the French wines produced from the sauvignon blanc and semillon grapes.

Pinot chardonnay, or simply chardonnay, is the state's best white wine. Growing in the coastal counties around San Francisco Bay, the chardonnay grape—also responsible for the great French white burgundies—develops a certain elegance, a light color, a good body, and a delicate, fragrant bouquet. The pinot blanc wines are similar to it but not as good. Chenin blanc is crisp and pleasant, somewhat sweeter than the Loire wines that are made from the same grape. The California wines bearing the names of the johannisberg riesling (or white riesling), riesling, grey riesling, sylvaner, and traminer grape varieties are light and fragrant, reminiscent of the rhine and moselle wines of Germany. The johannisberg riesling is nearest to German rieslings in character and delicacy. The traminer wines (now often called gewürztraminer) have a spicy, flowerlike perfume, with a resemblance to their Alsatian cousins. Grey riesling wines are least like German whites, but then, the grey riesling grape is a Californian varietal hybrid offshoot, developed for the hotter climate. Green hungarian is another unique variety produced in small quantity.

SOME RECOMMENDED CALIFORNIA VARIETAL WHITE WINES

Following are producers recommended by CU's consultants, graded into two categories. Occasional variants in the varietal names are noted.

CHARDONNAY or PINOT CHARDONNAY

Very Good ($2.65 to $4.20): Beaulieu, Inglenook, Robert Mondavi, Wente.

Good ($2.65 to $4.20): Almadén, Christian Brothers.

CHENIN BLANC

Very Good ($2.35 to $2.70): Christian Brothers, Inglenook, Mirassou, Robert Mondavi.

Good ($2.35 to $2.70): Charles Krug, Weibel, Wente "Blanc de Blancs."

GREEN HUNGARIAN

Good ($2.60 to $3): Buena Vista, Sebastiani, Weibel.

GREY RIESLING

Good ($2 to $2.65): Almadén, Beringer, Korbel, Wente.

JOHANNISBERG RIESLING

Very Good ($2.65 to $3.50): Beaulieu, Charles Krug.

Good ($2.65 to $3.50): Almadén, Weibel.

PINOT BLANC

Good ($2.60 to $3.50): Inglenook, Paul Masson, Wente.

SAUVIGNON BLANC (Dry, except as noted)

Good: ($2.45 to $3): Christian Brothers, Concannon, Charles Krug (semisweet), Robert Mondavi "Fumé Blanc," Wente.

SEMILLON (Dry, except as noted)

Good ($2.15 to $3.50): Almadén, Cresta Blanca "Premier Semillon," Charles Krug, Wente, Wente "Château Semillon" (sweet).

SYLVANER

Good ($1.95 to $2.60): Almadén, Charles Krug, Louis Martini, Paul Masson.

TRAMINER

Good ($2.35 to $2.65): Almadén "Gewürztraminer," Inglenook, Charles Krug "Gewürztraminer."

Generic white wines

Many generic-white producers in California do a remarkably good job, in the opinion of CU's consultants, particularly when price is considered. You may very well enjoy California's so-called "rhine" wines or "chablis" or "sauterne" if you don't compare them with their European counterparts. They are to be judged on their own terms as sound, pleasant wines from a non-European soil and climate. As with the reds, the generic whites are blended to be uniform from bottle to bottle. They are low in price and many come in larger-than-fifth bottles (some don't even come in fifths).

SOME RECOMMENDED CALIFORNIA GENERIC WHITE WINES

Following are producers of three generic white wines selected by CU's consultants. All of these are also produced in half-gallon and gallon sizes, though not necessarily both. Prices are given for all three sizes.

CHABLIS

Good ($1.15 to $2.05; half-gallon, $2.45 to $4.25; gallon, $4.40 to $7.85): Almadén Mountain White, Beringer Mountain Chablis, CK-Mondavi, Christian Brothers, Cresta Blanca, Gallo, Inglenook, Italian Swiss Colony, Louis Martini Mountain White, Paul Masson.

RHINE

Good ($1.15 to $2.05; half-gallon, $2.45 to $4.25; gallon, $4.40 to $7.85): Almadén Mountain White, CK-Mondavi, Christian Brothers, Cresta Blanca, Gallo, Inglenook, Italian Swiss Colony, Paul Masson.

SAUTERNE (Dry)

Good ($1.15 to $2; half-gallon, $2.45 to $4.25; gallon, $4.40 to $7.85): Almadén Mountain White, CK-Mondavi, Christian Brothers, Cresta Blanca, Gallo, Italian Swiss Colony, Paul Masson.

Proprietary white wines

Certain producers have given their own made-up names to blends of whites as they have for reds. Christian Brothers' Château La Salle, a sweet flowery wine, and Paul Masson's Emerald Dry, a soft white, are examples. Since these wines are quite individual, and hardly comparable to each other, CU's consultants did not make recommendations in this category. They list the following, in addition to the two above (producer's name in parentheses): Rhine Castle (Paul Masson), Château Masson (Paul Masson), Château Wente (Wente), Château Beaulieu (Beaulieu), Rhinegarten (Gallo), Vine Brook (Buena Vista).

WHITE WINES OF NEW YORK STATE

In general, CU's consultants consider the eastern white wines of higher quality than the eastern reds and feel there is great potential in the developments now taking place, especially in New York State. Experimentation with French-American hybrid vines and with vinifera varieties themselves is beginning to produce some interesting and surprising wines. This is the result of painfully slow and dedicated work on the part of both small vineyard proprietors and larger companies. Even the native varieties have been bred to lose some of their so-called "foxy" flavor (a pronounced grapey taste). The production in the East is concentrated primarily in New York State, with some in Ohio, Pennsylvania, and elsewhere.

Of the native varietals, three are perhaps the most interesting: catawba, semidry and full-flavored; delaware, fresh and spicy; and dutchess, light and dry. None taste much like European or even California wines, but each has its own distinctive flavor.

Many of the wines from the new French-American hybrids are being marketed under a vineyard's own proprietary name rather than the name of the hybrid, since the hybrids themselves are hardly known. Some of the better ones are listed in the suggestions below. The true vinifera varietals are still in very short supply, but CU's consultants feel they are so promising that they are definitely worth hunting for. Several are suggested below.

The eastern generic whites are quite good for what they are, some of them even preferable (say CU's consultants) to their California counterparts. However, they are not at all similar to their European namesakes and should be judged on their own merits, not on a comparison basis.

SOME SUGGESTED NEW YORK STATE WHITE WINES

Among the wines made from native varieties, our consultants suggest the catawbas from Gold Seal and Widmer, the dutchess from Great Western, and two proprietary-named wines, Taylor's Lake Country White and Widmer's Lake Niagara. These range from $1.50 to $2.15 and are also available in half-gallons. Among the wines made from French-American hybrids are Benmarl Vineyards Blanc Domaine, Boordy Vineyards White, Bully Hill White, Gold Seal's Charles Fournier Chablis Nature, and High Tor's Rockland White. These range from $1.90 to $3.75. Among the true vinifera varietals available are Gold Seal's Pinot Chardonnay ($2.75) and two from Dr. Konstantin Frank, Pinot Chardonnay and Johannisberger Riesling (both $4.50). Among the generic producers recommended by our consultants are Gold Seal, Great Western, Hudson Valley, Taylor, and Widmer. Most of them make chablis, rhine, and sauterne wines ranging from $1.80 to $2, and many of these wines also come in half-gallon bottles.

WHITE WINES FROM OTHER COUNTRIES

There are some lesser-known, less expensive, and worthy whites from countries other than those mentioned above. These wines are not, of course, in such wide distribution, but they can be found, particularly in a well-stocked wine shop. CU's consultants suggest looking for the following (brand name and price given in parentheses after the wine name).

From *Australia:* Rhymney Chablis (Seppelt, $2.70). From *Austria:* Gumpoldskirchner (Marienthaler, $2), Kremser (Schloss Kirchberg, $2.75). From *Chile:* Riesling (Concha y Toro, $1.60), Rhin (Undurraga, $2). From *Greece:* Santa Helena (Achaia, $2.15), Hymettus (Cambas, $2). From *Hungary:* Badacsonyi Szurkebarat, Csopaki Olaszrizling (both Export Monimpex, $3). From *Luxembourg:* Auxerrois (Grand Duché de Luxembourg, $2.95). From *Portugal:* Vinho Verde (Casal Garcia, $2.45). From *Spain:* Cepa de Oro (Bodegas Bilbainas, $2.35), Reserva Blanco (Marqués de Murrieta, $3). From *Switzerland:* Aigle (H. Badoux, $3.50), Dézaley (Grossenbacher, $4.25), Fendant (Gillard, $3.80), Neuchâtel (Châtenay, $3.25). From *Yugoslavia:* Sipon (Slovin, $1.80), Zupa Rizling (Navip, $1.80).

Chapter 6

~~~~~~

CHAMPAGNE

France is very strict about which of its wines may be called champagne. By law the name belongs exclusively to sparkling white wines that have undergone a natural secondary fermentation in the bottle and have been produced from grapes grown in certain areas of the former province of Champagne, most of which is now the department of the Marne. There is still, or nonsparkling, champagne, but it is called *vin nature de la champagne* (and is not very impressive and is not exported); and there is pink champagne (pink because the skins of red grapes were left in the vat long enough to tint the pressings), but it is called *champagne rosé* (and is held in much higher esteem by Americans than by the French). But only that pale, golden bubbly liquid long associated with caviar, early strawberries, ship christenings, and New Year's Eve is, simply, champagne.

The vineyards responsible for champagne are the most northerly of any associated with France's important wines and have a chalky-clay soil similar to that of the chablis region. In most of the vineyards red grapes, chiefly pinot noir, are cultivated, but in some are grown white grapes, chiefly chardonnay; and, in fact, champagne is usually a blend of the two, with the red grapes predominating. *Blancs de blancs* (white wines from white grapes) are becoming somewhat more common than they used to be, though they remain, as they have always been, expensive.

What makes all champagnes at least relatively expensive, though, is not the grapes so much as those little bubbles. Some sparkling wines are merely carbonated, like soda pop, and some—thanks to a process developed in 1910 by a Frenchman named Eugene Charmat—go through their second fermentation in large pressure tanks, but none of these wines, in France, can be called champagne. French champagne acquires its bubbles in the bottle, and because it does, its production is a difficult, time-consuming, and costly affair. It has been so since the "discovery" of champagne.

How it's made

Until late in the seventh century any wine that fermented again in the bottle either burst its container or ended up a still wine because the bottle's primitive oil-soaked cotton or cloth-and-wood stopper let the carbon dioxide gas escape. But then a Benedictine monk, Dom Pérignon, cellar-master at the Abbey of Hautvillers, decided that sparkling wines were worth saving. And save them he did by putting them in stronger bottles stopped by thick cork plugs that were tied down with string. He is also credited with being among the first to blend the wines of champagne in order to improve the final product.

Today most champagnes are blends; very few are *vins de cru*— *i.e.,* wines from grapes of only one locality. The *coupage,* or blending, takes place after the wines have gone through their first fermentation, in casks. It is a delicate operation, for part of the blender's job is to spot potential flaws or impurities in the raw wines he is tasting. Once blended, the wine is ready for its second fermentation; to ensure this, a solution of sugar dissolved in old wine is added to the new wine just before it is bottled.

The bottles are stacked on their sides in cellars cold enough so that the second fermentation may proceed at its own pace. Each year's vintage ferments for only a few months, from about April to July (in the year after the original harvest), but the bottles are left in the cellar beyond this period—two, three, perhaps four years—so that their contents may "ripen." Unfortunately, while the wine "ripens," sediment from the fermentation forms in the bottles. As a result, the wine requires *remuage* and *degorgement*.

Storing and Serving

Like all wines, champagne should be stored, both in the store and at home, on its side and, if possible, in a cool, dark place. Before it is served, it should be chilled in the refrigerator for three or four hours or in an ice bucket for about an hour. Don't let it get too cold, though, or you'll lose part of its flavor and aroma.

Remove the cork *slowly* to lessen the fizz and the wine loss, and hold onto it lest it become a dangerous missile. The best way is to hold the cork with one hand and turn the bottle with the other. This gives you the most leverage. *Don't* serve your champagne in those so-called "champagne" glasses, the wide-mouthed, shallow ones that were really meant for sherbert. Rather, use the general-purpose 8- or 9-ounce "tulip"-shaped glasses mentioned earlier—they preserve the bubbles longer than the wide-mouthed glasses do and collect the wine's bouquet for savoring.

Remuage means "shaking." Inserted in a sloping rack, first at an angle of about 30 degrees, the bottles are gradually, over a space of many days, raised to an upside down position. Every day, as their slant steepens, the *remuer* shakes them and gives them a slight turn. Ultimately all the sediment in each bottle slides down into the bottle's neck, where it comes to rest against the cork. *Degorgement* is now in order.

First the neck of the bottle is frozen by passing the bottle, neck down, through a trough of icy brine. Then the cork is eased out, and—*woosh!*—the built-up pressure in the bottle expels the sediment and a small quantity of wine in a solid icy lump. Aged wine from another bottle is added to the depleted bottle, and the product is ready for *dosage* and the insertion of a second and final cork.

Dosage is the practice of sweetening the wine with a little syrup made of sugar, wine, and brandy. Champagne comes in five sweetnesses (drynesses). The driest of them is termed *brut* in both French and English. Brut champagne, the regulations say, may contain no more than 1½ per cent sugar; *extra-sec,* or extra dry, is allowed no more than 2 per cent; and so on, through *sec* and *demi-sec,* all the way up to *doux,* or sweet, champagne, which may have as much as 10 per cent sugar (seldom, if ever, seen these days). Ordinarily the producer uses those wines he believes to be his finest for brut champagne, because the drier the wine, the easier to detect any defects it may have.

The last step of all is the return of the wine to the cellar for another term of routinely inspected aging. This period may last as long as two years, so that, all told, six or seven years is not an unusual length of time for the processing of a top-of-the-line champagne.

The American way

The United States is the only country which allows the use of the name "champagne" for a wine made outside the Champagne district of France. However, it does restrict use of the name. Federal law requires that American champagnes undergo a secondary fermentation in "glass containers" and, further, that they possess "the taste, aroma, and other characteristics generally attributed to champagne as made in the Champagne district of France." However, the regulations do allow two distinct departures from the *méthode champenoise,* as the true champagne process (described above) is known.

The first difference—and to some experts this seems to make little or no change in quality—is to purge the sediment from the wines by the so-called "transfer" process rather than by individual *degorgement.* With the transfer method, after the champagne has ripened, it is simply emptied into a pressure system, filtered free of sediment, and then put into fresh, clean bottles for the final aging. Producers using this system cannot say *fermented in this bottle* on the label (they say *in the bottle*), but are not required to state *transfer process* on their labels.

The second difference is that U.S. regulations allow the Charmat, or bulk, process (page 75) to be used for wine labeled *champagne* provided that the label carry the words *Charmat bulk process* or *bulk process*. All American champagnes must in any case carry the words *American* or a state name (California or New York, usually) in large type to prevent confusion with France's product. (If a wine is artificially carbonated, it cannot be called "champagne," even in this country, but must be called "carbonated wine" or some equivalent.)

It pays then, to read domestic labels carefully if you're bent on buying American champagne made the French way. But you may be less interested in how the American product is processed than in how closely it resembles the French in bouquet and flavor. This was one of the questions CU set out to explore when it rounded up eleven expert wine tasters to judge forty-five nationally distributed wines, twenty-one French and twenty-four domestic. As far as we could, we limited our purchases to products labeled brut or extra dry. Two of the California champagnes and seven of the French were vintage wines and included two blancs de blancs, one from each country. Prices for CU's selections ranged from $4.44 to $17.98 for a bottle of 26—or roughly 26—fluid ounces.

Our tests and their results

Our blind-tasting sessions were conducted in the private rooms of a distinguished New York City restaurant, where we could be assured that the wines would be properly handled and served. At each session each taster was asked to judge five coded samples, among which were undifferentiated entries from France, California, and New York State. The experts' assignment was to compare these wines with one another; to score them for bouquet and flavor, degrees of dryness and bubble (the amount of carbonation), and overall quality; and, finally, to guess the place of origin of each of them.

The most notable finding of our tests was that all the experts preferred most of the French champagnes to any of the domestics. True, nearly half of the wines in the all-French top Ratings group were occasionally guessed to be domestic, but the tasters liked them —wherever they thought they came from.

At the same time, of the sixteen high-scoring French wines none was considered markedly better than another, and so all of them were rated superior in overall quality. As it turned out, among these sixteen were both the most expensive French wine tested and the *least* expensive, Mercier Extra Dry ($7.69).

The five remaining French wines ended up, along with five domestics, in the second of the four quality-performance groups, and were guessed to be non-French just about as often as not.

All but one of the French champagnes were judged brut—whatever dryness designation they may have been assigned by their label. On the other hand, only four domestics were considered brut; all four came from California, and among them Almadén Blanc de Blancs 1964 was highest-rated.

Interestingly, it didn't seem to matter very much to our experts how the twenty-four domestic wines had been fermented. In the second Ratings group, along with the five French wines, were two domestics labeled as having been *fermented in this bottle*, two as having been *fermented in the bottle,* and one, The Christian Brothers Brut, as having been fermented by the *Charmat bulk process.*

It is also worth noting that in the second Ratings group was only one New York State wine, Great Western Brut, and that the two lowest-rated champagnes in the project were from New York. Moreover, labels to the contrary, none of the New York State wines was judged brut. As it happens, grapes used in French and California production are usually varieties of the same red and white species (vinifera), whereas most grapes used to make New York State champagne are of an entirely different species (labrusca).

The vintage champagnes

About the vintage champagnes tested: A "vintage" year in France's champagne area is one whose weather promotes the growth of superior grapes. The resulting high-quality wine is then year-labeled on the bottle. In other years the wine is a blend of two or more years' production and is not year-labeled. Since the climate of California is more consistent, year-labeling is more the result of a producer's policy than the vagaries of the weather. In France the most recent vintage years have been 1959 (but its wines are starting to go off now—become darker and lose taste—as champagnes more than ten years old usually do), 1961, 1962, 1964, 1966, and 1969 (1970 and 1971 will probably be judged vintage years but this is not yet confirmed). Of course, most French champagne sold here is N.V. (non-vintage).

Of the seven French vintage wines we bought, three were '61s and four were '62s. Both of the California vintage wines tested were '64s. The showing of these nine wines in the Ratings does not provide a very clear-cut picture. Two of the seven French products —both '62s—failed to qualify for the top Ratings group, and one of the '64 Californians didn't make it to even the second group. The only thing, then, that we can say for certain about vintage wines is that they carry a higher-than-usual price tag.

What to buy

If you like the dry taste of French champagne, and if—a big "if"— either of the two Mercier offerings is distributed in your area, by all means try it. The experts put both on virtually an equal footing with the $17.98 Taittinger Comtes de Champagne Blanc de Blancs Brut 1961. Of course, if you're out to impress someone, you can hardly go wrong with the latter wine. It's the product of a great vintage year; it was made from white grapes only; and it comes in a *very* fancy bottle.

Otherwise, if domestic champagne is to your taste, we suggest you start with The Christian Brothers Brut. At $4.69 it costs a respectable amount less than even the $7.69 Mercier. If you want to give yourself a choice, note that there were two other American champagnes, both under $5, that were rated by our taste panel as being the equal of some rather famous names in the second quality group.

Ratings of Champagne

Listed by groups in order of estimated overall quality; within groups, listed in order of increasing price. Comments represent the consensus of subjective judgments made by a panel of expert tasters. Domestic wines are California or New York State products and so designated. Except when the vintage year is stated,* all are non-vintage wines. Prices per bottle (26 ounces or close to it) are New York State recommended retail prices as of June 1, 1972. Local prices may differ, but price relationships among the brands should be the same.

ACCEPTABLE

The following, all French, were judged superior in overall quality.

MERCIER EXTRA DRY (Dennis & Huppert Co., N.Y.C.), $7.69. Judged brut. Flavor and bouquet judged good to very good.

MERCIER BRUT (Dennis & Huppert Co.), $8.15. Judged brut. Flavor and bouquet judged good to very good.

LANSON BLACK LABEL BRUT (Schenley Import Co., N.Y.C.), $8.55. Judged extra dry to brut. Flavor judged good to very good; bouquet judged fair to good.

MOET & CHANDON WHITE SEAL EXTRA DRY (Schiefflin & Co., N.Y.C.), $8.99. Judged brut. Flavor judged good to very good; bouquet judged fair to good.

CHARLES HEIDSIECK BRUT (Austin, Nichols & Co., Inc., N.Y.C.), $9.19. Judged brut. Flavor judged good to very good; bouquet judged fair to good.

TAITTINGER LA FRANCAISE BRUT (Kobrand Corp., N.Y.C.), $9.49. Judged brut. Flavor and bouquet judged good to very good.

G. H. MUMM CORDON ROUGE BRUT (Browne Vintners Co., N.Y.C.), $9.75. Judged brut. Flavor judged good; bouquet judged fair to good.

VEUVE CLICQUOT PONSARDIN YELLOW LABEL BRUT (The Jos. Garneau Co., N.Y.C.), $9.75. Judged brut. Flavor and bouquet judged good to very good.

MOET & CHANDON IMPERIAL BRUT (Schiefflin & Co.), $9.85. Judged brut. Flavor judged good to very good; bouquet judged fair to good.

---

* Most of the vintage champagnes included in this test were from the years 1961 and 1962, now in very short supply. Later vintage years are, of course, being sold by the same companies, but since these were not tested, CU cannot say whether they would rank the same as the specific vintages shown. Current non-vintage champagnes should rank the same as those tested.

BOLLINGER BRUT (Julius Wile Sons & Co., N.Y.C.), $9.95. Judged brut. Flavor and bouquet judged good to very good.

LANSON RED LABEL BRUT 1961 (Schenley Import Co.), $10.25. Judged brut. Flavor and bouquet judged good to very good.

PIPER-HEIDSIECK CUVEE DES AMBASSADEURS BRUT (Renfield Importers, Ltd., Union, N.J.), $10.55. Judged brut. Flavor and bouquet judged good to very good.

VEUVE CLICQUOT PONSARDIN YELLOW LABEL BRUT (The Jos. Garneau Co.), $11.50. Judged brut. Flavor and bouquet judged good to very good.

PIPER-HEIDSIECK BRUT 1962 (Renfield Importers, Ltd.), $11.99. Judged brut. Flavor judged good; bouquet judged fair to good.

MOET & CHANDON CUVEE DOM PERIGNON 1961 (Schiefflin & Co.), $17.89. Judged brut. Flavor and bouquet judged good to very good.

TAITTINGER COMTES DE CHAMPAGNE BLANC DE BLANCS BRUT 1961 (Kobrand Corp.), $17.98. Judged brut. Flavor and bouquet judged good to very good.

The following wines were judged appreciably lower in overall quality than those preceding.

THE CHRISTIAN BROTHERS BRUT CALIFORNIA (The Christian Brothers, Napa, Calif.), $4.69. Judged extra dry to brut. Flavor judged mediocre to fair; bouquet judged fair to good.

ALMADEN BRUT CALIFORNIA (Almadén Vineyards, Los Gatos, Calif.), $4.96. Judged sec to extra dry. Flavor judged mediocre to fair; bouquet judged fair to good.

GREAT WESTERN BRUT NEW YORK STATE (Pleasant Valley Wine Co., Hammondsport, N.Y.), $4.99. Judged extra dry to brut. Flavor and bouquet judged fair to good.

KORBEL EXTRA DRY CALIFORNIA (F. Korbel and Bros., Inc., Sonoma County, Calif.), $5.25. Judged extra dry to brut. Flavor and bouquet judged fair to good.

ALMADEN BLANC DE BLANCS 1964 CALIFORNIA (Almadén Vineyards), $6.49. Judged brut. Flavor and bouquet judged fair to good.

G. H. MUMM EXTRA DRY (Browne Vintners Co.), $8.99. Judged brut. Flavor judged good to very good; bouquet fair to good.

PIPER-HEIDSIECK EXTRA DRY (Renfield Importers Ltd.), $9.75. Judged brut. Flavor and bouquet judged fair to good.

KRUG RESERVE BRUT (Seggerman Slocum, Inc., N.Y.C.), $9.75. Judged brut. Flavor judged good; bouquet fair to good.

BOLLINGER BRUT 1962 (Julius Wile Sons & Co.), $10.25. Judged brut. Flavor judged good; bouquet judged fair to good.

G. H. MUMM CORDON ROUGE BRUT 1962 (Browne Vintners Co.), $11.40. Judged brut. Flavor and bouquet judged fair to good.

The following wines were judged somewhat lower in overall quality than those preceding.

WIDMER BRUT NEW YORK STATE (Widmer's Wine Cellars, Inc., Naples, N.Y.), $4.45. Judged sec to extra dry. Flavor and bouquet judged mediocre to fair.

WIDMER EXTRA DRY NEW YORK STATE (Widmer's Wine Cellars, Inc.), $4.45. Judged sec. Flavor and bouquet judged mediocre to fair.

THE CHRISTIAN BROTHERS EXTRA DRY CALIFORNIA (The Christian Brothers), $4.69. Judged extra dry to brut. Flavor and bouquet judged fair to good.

GOLD SEAL ORANGE LABEL BRUT NEW YORK STATE (Gold Seal Vineyards, Inc., Hammondsport, N.Y.), $4.70. Judged extra dry to brut. Flavor and bouquet judged mediocre to fair.

GOLD SEAL WHITE LABEL EXTRA DRY NEW YORK STATE (Gold Seal Vineyards, Inc.), $4.70. Judged sec to extra dry. Flavor and bouquet judged mediocre to fair. More carbonated than any other champagne tested.

COOK'S IMPERIAL AMERICAN BRUT CALIFORNIA (American Wine Co., Fresno, Calif.), $4.85. Judged extra dry to brut. Flavor judged mediocre to fair; bouquet judged fair to good.

COOK'S IMPERIAL AMERICAN EXTRA DRY CALIFORNIA (American Wine Co.), $4.85. Judged sec to extra dry. Flavor and bouquet judged mediocre to fair.

TAYLOR WHITE LABEL DRY NEW YORK STATE (The Taylor Wine Co., Hammondsport, N.Y.), $4.90. Judged sec to extra dry. Flavor judged mediocre to fair; bouquet judged fair to good.

TAYLOR YELLOW LABEL BRUT NEW YORK STATE (The Taylor Wine Co.), $4.90. Judged extra dry to brut. Flavor and bouquet judged mediocre to fair.

ALMADEN EXTRA DRY CALIFORNIA (Almadén Vineyards), $4.96. Judged sec to extra dry. Flavor and bouquet judged fair to good.

GREAT WESTERN WHITE LABEL EXTRA DRY NEW YORK STATE (Pleasant Valley Wine Co.), $4.99. Judged sec to extra dry. Flavor and bouquet judged mediocre to fair.

PAUL MASSON BLACK LABEL EXTRA DRY CALIFORNIA (Paul Masson Vineyards, Saratoga, Calif.), $5.09. Judged brut. Flavor judged mediocre to fair; bouquet judged fair to good.

PAUL MASSON BRUT CALIFORNIA (Paul Masson Vineyards), $5.09. Judged brut. Flavor judged mediocre to fair; bouquet judged fair to good.

HANNS KORNELL BRUT CALIFORNIA (Hanns Kornell Champagne

Cellars, St. Helena, Calif.), $5.20. Judged extra dry to brut. Flavor and bouquet judged mediocre to fair.

HANNS KORNELL EXTRA DRY CALIFORNIA (Hanns Kornell Champagne Cellars), $5.20. Judged extra dry to brut. Flavor and bouquet judged fair to good.

KORBEL BRUT CALIFORNIA (F. Korbel and Bros., Inc.), $5.25. Judged brut. Flavor and bouquet judged mediocre to fair.

BEAULIEU BV BRUT 1964 CALIFORNIA (Beaulieu Vineyard, Rutherford, Calif.), $5.63. Judged dry to brut. Flavor judged mediocre to fair; bouquet judged fair to good.

The following two wines were judged decidedly lower in overall quality than those preceding.

DRY IMPERATOR WHITE LABEL EXTRA DRY NEW YORK STATE (Robin Fils & Cie, Ltd., Batavia, N.Y.), $4.44. Judged extra dry to brut. Flavor and bouquet judged mediocre.

IMPERATOR BLACK LABEL BRUT NEW YORK STATE (Robin Fils & Cie, Ltd.), $4.80. Judged extra dry to brut. Flavor and bouquet judged mediocre to fair. Less carbonated than any champagne tested.

Chapter 7

FORTIFIED WINES

The term "dessert wine" as applied to port and sherry isn't entirely apt. First of all, it makes no allowance for the fact that *dry* sherry is usually served before, not at the end of, a meal; and, secondly, it lumps port and sherry with wines essentially different from them—sweet table wines such as sauternes and tokay. United States regulations prohibit use of the term "fortified wine" on wine labels but fortified wine (*i.e.,* wine whose alcoholic content has been raised by additional alcohol above its natural limit of around 14 per cent) is what port and sherry are—and what ordinary table wines are not. (The extra alcohol preserves the wine after the bottle has been opened. There is no need to chill the bottle, as with table wines.)

In this country, sherry—dry, sweet, and in between—is the most popular of fortified wines, followed not very closely by port. Far behind either of them in sales are marsala (a sweet fortified wine from Sicily, used a good deal in cooking), malaga (from Spain and quite overshadowed by its compatriot sherry), and madeira (from the Portuguese island of Madeira). The last-named wine used to be an American favorite (in colonial times), but has only lately begun to spark interest again. It is available in several distinct types (each made from a different grape variety) ranging from verdelho and sercial, which are dry and often light-bodied, to malmsey and boal, which are deep gold, sweet, and full-bodied, much fancied by the Victorians with a biscuit or a piece of cake.

Of these several wines, we tested only the relatively important sellers: port, dry sherry, and sweet sherry. Our panel of expert wine tasters subjected imported and domestic brands of each category to blind tastings. The samples they sipped were anonymous and coded, and some of them were secret duplicates of the same brand—checks, as it were, on our panelists' consistency. Character, sweetness, aroma, freedom from flaws, and conformity to type were the factors for which each sample was judged. Because the imported brands come in various-sized bottles instead of fifths as domestics do, we give in the Ratings, when necessary, their equivalent price per fifth; actual prices and sizes are noted in parentheses.

PORT

According to Federal law, port from California must be called California port and port from New York must be called New York port, and so on. But port from Portugal—the true and original port, shipped from the city of Porto, or Oporto, and produced in a strictly delimited area along the Douro River—need be called only port. However, the Portuguese are turning more and more to the use of the word oporto, which can only mean port from Portugal.

Port wine as we know it came into existence in the eighteenth century, when, in order to make Portuguese red wine a better traveler, its producers began to fortify it with up to 20 per cent Portuguese grape brandy. The extra alcohol not only strengthened the wine but also, by halting its fermentation before all the sugar in it had been fermented, made it sweeter. The result was perhaps a shade too rich and full-bodied for a warm country such as Portugal, which keeps less than 10 per cent of its port for home consumption, but just right, apparently, for a colder part of the world such as England, which today still largely accounts for—and to some extent controls—the sale of port.

Styles of port

Port is made from several grape varieties, all grown in vineyards that cling to the steep slopes of the Upper Douro's gorge. Some mechanization has been introduced into its production, but the grapes are still tended and picked mostly by hand. Some are still trodden out on stone pressing floors.

After it has been allowed to ferment for a few days, the wine is run into casks containing brandy. Depending on when it is mixed with the wine and in what per cent, the brandy, stopping the fermentation, preserves as much of what remains of the grapes' sugar as the producer chooses to save. When the wine has settled, the casks are shipped to Oporto. They are stored in wine lodges at Vila Nova de Gaia, just across the river, where they are periodically refreshed with new wine and new brandy and eventually classified. Depending on the character of the wine, it is drawn off and bottled after varying periods of aging.

Young port wine is known as ruby port because of its deep purple-red color. A good ruby port is very fruity and fresh. The youngest Portuguese ruby is about six years old and is actually a blend of a number of ports mixed by the shipper to produce a flavor that he hopes will vary little from year to year.

Ruby is the least expensive port. Tawny port, lighter-bodied and less fruity than ruby, is the next step up. It is called tawny because in the ten to fifteen years or so that it is supposed to mature in the cask its color becomes darkly golden. True tawny port is comparatively expensive owing to its age, but much of the "tawny" available today is neither very expensive nor very old. In fact, it isn't true tawny, being merely a youngish blend of red and white port. (White port is made from white grapes and may be sweet or dry. Sweet, it has little market outside of France; dry, it is being publicized as an aperitif.) CU has no way of knowing which of the tested brands are genuine tawnys and which are not, but it is worth noting that most of the tawny ports tested cost no more than the rubys. Among the brands that do show a price difference between the two labeled types, only the domestic Louis Martini and the imported Harvey's brands offered tawnys that were judged to match their extra cost with extra quality.

The second-highest rung of the port hierarchy is occupied by crusted port, which is ruby bottled within a few years of its vintage and aged in the bottle—rather than in the cask—for perhaps twenty years. During this period the wine achieves elegance and finesse as it fades, loses body, and forms a crust, or deposit, around the bottle's interior.

Lastly there is vintage port, finest and most expensive port of all. A vintage port is handled like a crusted port—that is, aged in the bottle—but is the product of what the producer considers to have been an exceptional year for his grapes. The date of that year appears on the bottle's label.

Tests and results

A bottle of crusted or vintage port is likely to be very expensive, and, because of the sediment it contains, must be carefully decanted before it can be drunk—something of a chore for the amateur. Not surprisingly, very little crusted or vintage port is sold in this country—and none was included in CU's tests. Of the forty-eight brands of port we did buy, some were labeled *tawny*, some were labeled *ruby*, and some were labeled just plain *port*. Eight of them were from Portugal, twenty-nine were from California, nine were from New York, and two were from Ohio.

We were curious to learn whether not-*very*-expensive Portuguese ports were readily distinguishable from some of our often quite *in*expensive domestic ports. We discovered that, by and large, they were not. It's true that the one brand top-rated Good-to-Very Good by our expert tasters was a Portuguese tawny selling at $5.15 a fifth and that the four bottom-rated brands were all low- or lowish-priced domestics. But three of the four wines rated Good were domestics, too, and six of the eight Portuguese brands tested (three rubys, three tawnys) wound up below them, in the Fair-to-Good category.

Whether your own "ratings" of the brands tested would agree with the experts' we cannot say. Not only do tastes differ, but the wines themselves differ, in taste as well as in quality. (Meier's

Tawny, for instance, was found to be "very sweet"; all the other brands were considered "sweet.") It's a fair bet, though, that if you're the average port sipper, you're not going to find four dollars worth of difference between Good-to-Very Good Harvey's Fine Tawny Hunting Port and merely Good Roma Reserve California Tawny Port.

From another point of view, at 96 cents a fifth, Roma Tawny may seem especially desirable to you if you compare it with the six Portuguese brands rated lower than it and ranging in price from $2.65 to $6.19 a bottle. Incidentally, both Roma Reserve California Ruby Port, which was rated Fair-to-Good, and Roma Reserve California Port, which was rated only Fair, cost the same as Roma Tawny.

As to the serving of port—or, for that matter, sherry, sweet or dry—CU's consultants recommend the same basic tulip-shaped wine glass they suggest for table wines and champagnes, with a little less fill to balance the extra strength. Designs for such glasses are shown on page 14.

Ratings of Ports

Listed by groups in order of estimated overall quality, based on judgments of CU's expert taste panel, and within groups by increasing price. Prices (per fifth) for national brands are recommended retail prices for New York State; for private-label brands, those paid by CU's shoppers; for other sizes, the cost equivalent of a fifth (actual size and price are then shown parenthetically). Prices may differ in other states, but their relationship among brands should be similar.

ACCEPTABLE—Good-to-Very Good
HARVEY'S FINE TAWNY HUNTING PORT (Heublein, Inc., Hartford, Conn.), $5.27 ($5.15 for 25 oz.). Portuguese.

ACCEPTABLE—Good
ROMA RESERVE CALIFORNIA TAWNY PORT (Roma Wine Co., Fresno, Calif.), 96¢ ($1.20 a quart).

WIDMER NEW YORK STATE TAWNY PORT (Widmer's Wine Cellars, Inc., Naples, N.Y.), $1.95.

LOUIS M. MARTINI CALIFORNIA TAWNY PORT (Louis M. Martini, St. Helena, Calif.), $3.15.

HARVEY'S GOLD CAP FINE RUBY PORT (Heublein, Inc.), $4.09 ($3.99 for 25 oz.). Portuguese.

ACCEPTABLE—Fair-to-Good

ROMA RESERVE CALIFORNIA RUBY PORT (Roma Wine Co.), 96¢ ($1.20 a quart).

COAST TO COAST CALIFORNIA PORT (Private-label brand for A&P Stores), 97¢.

COAST TO COAST CALIFORNIA TAWNY PORT (A&P), 97¢.

GALLO CALIFORNIA PORT (Gallo Vineyards, Modesto, Calif.), $1 ($1.25 a quart).

GALLO CALIFORNIA RUBY PORT (Gallo Vineyards), $1 ($1.25 a quart).

PETRI CRYSTAL PURE CALIFORNIA PORT (Petri Wineries, Newark, N.J.), $1.

PETRI CRYSTAL PURE CALIFORNIA TAWNY PORT (Petri Wineries), $1.

ITALIAN SWISS COLONY CALIFORNIA PORT (Italian Swiss Colony, Newark, N.J.), $1.10.

ITALIAN SWISS COLONY CALIFORNIA TAWNY PORT (Italian Swiss Colony), $1.10.

RED STAR PRIVATE STOCK CALIFORNIA PORT (Private-label brand for R. H. Macy & Co., Inc., N.Y.C.), $1.10.

RED STAR PRIVATE STOCK CALIFORNIA TAWNY PORT (R. H. Macy & Co., Inc.), $1.10.

GALLO OLD DECANTER BRAND CALIFORNIA TAWNY PORT (Gallo Vineyards), $1.25.

BRISTOL CLUB NEW YORK STATE TAWNY PORT (Private-label brand for Gimbel Bros., Inc., N.Y.C.), $1.29.

PAUL MASSON CALIFORNIA RICH RUBY PORT (Paul Masson Vineyards, Saratoga, Calif.), $1.80.

PAUL MASSON CALIFORNIA TAWNY PORT (Paul Masson Vineyards), $1.80.

GOLD SEAL NEW YORK STATE RUBY PORT (Gold Seal Vineyards, Inc., Hammondsport, N.Y.), $1.85.

GOLD SEAL NEW YORK STATE TAWNY PORT (Gold Seal Vineyards, Inc.), $1.85.

THE CHRISTIAN BROTHERS PURE CALIFORNIA RUBY PORT (The Christian Bros., Napa, Calif.), $1.90.

THE CHRISTIAN BROTHERS PURE CALIFORNIA TAWNY PORT (The Christian Bros.), $1.90.

ALMADEN CALIFORNIA SOLERA TINTA RUBY PORT (Almadén Vineyards, Los Gatos, Calif.), $1.92.

ALMADEN CALIFORNIA SOLERA TINTA TAWNY PORT (Almadén Vineyards), $1.92.

BERINGER NAPA VALLEY CALIFORNIA PORT (Beringer Bros., Inc., St. Helena, Calif.), $1.94.

TAYLOR NEW YORK STATE PORT WINE (The Taylor Wine Co., Inc., Hammondsport, N.Y.), $1.94.

TAYLOR NEW YORK STATE TAWNY PORT WINE (The Taylor Wine Co., Inc.), $1.94.

WIDMER NEW YORK STATE RUBY PORT (Widmer's Wine Cellars, Inc.), $1.95.

CRESTA BLANCA CALIFORNIA PORT (Cresta Blanca Vineyards, San Francisco), $1.98.

CRESTA BLANCA CALIFORNIA TAWNY PORT (Cresta Blanca Vineyards), $1.98.

BV CALIFORNIA PORT (Beaulieu Vineyard, Rutherford, Calif.), $1.99.

GREAT WESTERN NEW YORK STATE PORT (Pleasant Valley Wine Co., Hammondsport, N.Y.), $1.99.

MEIER'S RUBY RED OHIO STATE PORT (Meier's Wine Cellars, Inc., Silverton, Ohio), $1.99.

MEIER'S OHIO STATE TAWNY PORT (Meier's Wine Cellars, Inc.), $1.99.

YORK HOUSE RUBY FINE PORT WINE (R. H. Macy & Co., Inc.), $2.71 ($2.65 for 25 oz.). Portuguese.

YORK HOUSE TAWNY FINE PORT WINE (R. H. Macy & Co., Inc.), $2.71 ($2.65 for 25 oz.). Portuguese.

PAUL MASSON RARITY CALIFORNIA RARE TAWNY PORT (Paul Masson Vineyards), $3.

LOUIS M. MARTINI CALIFORNIA PORT (Louis M. Martini), $3.15.

SANDEMAN RUBY PORT (W. A. Taylor & Co., N.Y.C.), $3.99. Portuguese.

SANDEMAN TAWNY PORT (W. A. Taylor & Co.), $3.99. Portuguese.

COCKBURN NO. 25 DARK RUBY PORT (Munson G. Shaw Co., N.Y.C.), $4.79. Portuguese.

COCKBURN NO. 85 DRY CHOICE TAWNY CLUB PORT (Munson G. Shaw Co.), $6.19. Portuguese.

ACCEPTABLE—Fair

ROMA RESERVE CALIFORNIA PORT (Roma Wine Co.), 96¢ ($1.20 a quart).

PETRI CRYSTAL PURE CALIFORNIA RUBY PORT (Petri Wineries), $1.

ACCEPTABLE—Fair-to-Poor

ITALIAN SWISS COLONY CALIFORNIA RUBY PORT (Italian Swiss Colony), $1.10.

GREAT WESTERN NEW YORK STATE TAWNY PORT (Pleasant Valley Wine Co.), $1.99.

SHERRY

Sherry—or sack, as the Elizabethans called it—comes from vineyards around the Spanish town of Jerez-de-la-Frontera, or simply Jerez. It also comes from California, New York, and Ohio. Like port, sherry is a wine that can cost you as much as $5 (or more) per imported bottle—or as little as $1 for a domestic fifth. Is there a real difference in quality between the imports and the domestics? And if the imports do have the edge, is their superiority worth the price you must pay for it? To look into these questions CU conducted two separate sherry-tasting projects, one for each of the basic types of sherry: pale dry (called *fino*) and sweeter full-bodied (called *oloroso*).

Styles of sherry

The dry finos are generally drunk as aperitifs. Included in this category are *manzanillas,* which are very dry, very pale, and light-bodied; *finos* (again), which are very dry, very pale, and light-to-medium-bodied; and *amontillados,* which are dry, usually light golden, nutty-flavored, and medium-to-full-bodied.

Olorosos, like port, are generally served with or after dessert. They are naturally dry, but we who live out of Spain usually get them after they have been sweetened. All are full-bodied and nutty. They include *amorosos,* which are golden and medium-sweet; *olorosos* (again), which are deep golden and, most often, sweet; *creams,* which are deep golden and sweet to very sweet; and *browns,* which are dark brown and very sweet. As the names of the last two groups seem to suggest, it was the English who made sweet sherry popular.

Making sherry

Sherry ferments violently at first, for about a week, then calms down to a steadier pace for a few months, during which time it "falls bright"—the insolubles in it sink to the bottom of the cask. Clarified and almost totally dry, the raw wine, by virtue of a strange phenomenon, is now ready for its first, broad classification: fino or oloroso? If it has developed a surface veil of *flor,* an airborne yeast of the region, it's on its way to being a fino. If it hasn't, it will be an oloroso. The odd and inexplicable thing is that, of two casks of wine pressed the same day from the same grape harvest, one may go one way and one the other.

Classification follows classification: While they age in their *criaderas* (nurseries), the potential finos and olorosos are subtyped and graded for quality. Then the time comes when they are ready for the *solera,* a blending system designed to afford the shipper a virtually bottomless barrel of constant-quality sherry. A solera consists of tiers of wine casks; the wines in a particular solera differ in age, but all are of the same style, character, and quality. Wine drawn from casks in the oldest tier (at the lowest level) is replaced by wine from the next oldest (just above it), and so on up the tiers. The whole process, from youngest tier to oldest, takes just as long as it took to lay down the solera originally—sometimes as much as seven years—and all along the way the older wine forms and "educates" the younger.

For the olorosos, blending continues even after they have left their soleras. In some instances they are blended with stock from other soleras, and if they are meant for export, they are apt to be sweetened, usually with a thick, black blending wine called Pedro Ximenez, after the raisined grape from which it was made. Finally, wine brandy is added to the olorosos to bring them up to a maximum of 21 per cent alcohol. (The lightest finos contain as little as 14 per cent, barely enough to warrant calling them fortified.)

Because of all the blending it undergoes, a sherry is known neither by its vineyard nor by its vintage. Occasionally you will find *Solera 1847* or some such legend on a sherry label. But what it signifies is that the solera was founded in 1847, not that the wine is of 1847 vintage (although a tiny fraction of it may be).

Tests and results

Domestic sherries are made to correspond to the various types produced in Jerez—"cocktail" or "dry," for example, is our way of saying "fino." But CU's wine tasters discovered that, in some of the sherry categories, the relation between the Spanish and the similarly named American products was rather tenuous. This is not necessarily to imply that some American sherries are mediocre *wines,* but that they are mediocre *sherries.* If their makers had not called them "sherry," our consultants might well have thought more highly of them.

Again working with anonymous, coded, and sometimes duplicate samples, the panelists, in separate projects, taste-tested nineteen domestic and seven imported dry sherries and twenty-two domestic and eight imported sweet sherries. Their judgments concerning the sweet group may save you a fair amount of money over the years if you're a sweet-sherry drinker: Two of the three brands they top-rated Good were domestic and cost about $2, as compared to $4.85 for a bottle of the third brand, an import. Even many of the other domestics cost more than these two brands.

With the dry sherries it was a somewhat different story. Of the six top-rated brands (all judged Good), four were Spanish; and one of the domestics, the $1.39 Bristol Club New York State, is not nationally distributed, being a private-label brand of Gimbels department store in New York City. However, Gold Seal New York State Cocktail Sherry, the $1.85 brand, *is* widely available.

Among the dry sherries, none was considered unduly sweet; but neither was any judged really dry, although three Spanish brands— York House Manzanilla, Pedro Domecq La Ina, and Harvey's Bristol Fino—came close. Among the three top-rated sweet sherries, the one found least sweet was the California brand, and the one found most sweet was the brand from Spain. Thus, although the judges rated all three brands equal in overall quality, they did not find them identical in taste with one another. If you were to sample each member of the trio to find out which you yourself preferred, chances are that the total tab would run little more than a dollar and a half more than you'd pay for a bottle of famous Harvey's Bristol Cream, which was rated only Fair-to-Good, its price of $7.15 notwithstanding.

Sweet sherry is traditionally served, like port, at room temperature, but a dry sherry, used as an aperitif, may be served quite respectably chilled or on-the-rocks. Indeed, the American addiction to drinks on-the-rocks has spread even to sweet sherry so you will not be alone if you try it on ice.

Ratings of Sherries

Within types, listed by groups in order of estimated overall quality, based on judgments of CU's expert taste panel, and within groups by increasing price. Prices (per fifths) for national brands are recommended retail for New York State; for private-label brands, those paid by CU's shoppers; for other sizes, the cost equivalent of a fifth (actual size and price are then shown parenthetically); prices may differ in other states, but their relationship among brands should be similar.

DRY SHERRIES

ACCEPTABLE—Good

BRISTOL CLUB NEW YORK STATE COCKTAIL SHERRY (Private-label brand for Gimbel Bros., Inc., N.Y.C.), $1.39.

GOLD SEAL NEW YORK STATE COCKTAIL SHERRY (Gold Seal Vineyards, Inc., Hammondsport, N.Y.), $1.85.

YORK HOUSE MANZANILLA VERY DRY SHERRY (Private-label brand for R. H. Macy & Co., Inc., N.Y.C.), $3.07 ($3 for 25 oz.). Spanish.

HARVEY'S MEDIUM DRY AMONTILLADO COCKTAIL SHERRY (Heublein, Inc., Hartford, Conn.), $4.09 ($3.99 for 25 oz.). Spanish.

DUFF GORDON CLUB DRY AMONTILLADO SHERRY (Munson G. Shaw Co., N.Y.C.), $4.76 ($4.65 for 25 oz.). Spanish.

DRY SACK SHERRY (Julius Wile Sons & Co., Inc., N.Y.C.), $5.10 ($4.98 for 25 oz.). Spanish.

ACCEPTABLE—Fair-to-Good

ROMA RESERVE CALIFORNIA EXTRA DRY COCKTAIL SHERRY (Roma Wine Co., Fresno, Calif.), 96¢ ($1.20 a quart).

COAST TO COAST CALIFORNIA PALE DRY COCKTAIL SHERRY (Private-label brand for A&P Stores), 97¢.

GALLO COCKTAIL SHERRY PALE DRY (California) (Gallo Vineyards, Modesto, Calif.), $1 ($1.25 a quart).

PETRI CRYSTAL PURE CALIFORNIA COCKTAIL SHERRY (Petri Wineries, Newark, N.J.), $1.

ITALIAN SWISS COLONY CALIFORNIA COCKTAIL PALE DRY SHERRY (Italian Swiss Colony, Newark, N.J.), $1.10.

RED STAR PRIVATE STOCK CALIFORNIA COCKTAIL SHERRY (R. H. Macy & Co., Inc.), $1.10.

PAUL MASSON CALIFORNIA COCKTAIL SHERRY (Paul Masson Vineyards, Saratoga, Calif.), $1.80.

THE CHRISTIAN BROTHERS PURE CALIFORNIA COCKTAIL SHERRY PALE DRY (The Christian Bros., Napa, Calif.), $1.90.

ALMADEN CALIFORNIA SOLERA COCKTAIL SHERRY (Almadén Vineyards, Los Gatos, Calif.), $1.92.

TAYLOR NEW YORK STATE PALE DRY COCKTAIL SHERRY (The Taylor Wine Co., Inc., Hammondsport, N.Y.), $1.94.

WIDMER VERY PALE & DRY NEW YORK STATE COCKTAIL SHERRY (Widmer's Wine Cellars, Inc., Naples, N.Y.), $1.95.

CRESTA BLANCA CALIFORNIA PALOMINO PALE DRY SHERRY (Cresta Blanca Vineyards, San Francisco), $1.98.

BV CALIFORNIA PALE DRY SHERRY (Beaulieu Vineyard, Rutherford, Calif.), $1.99.

GREAT WESTERN NEW YORK STATE PALE DRY COCKTAIL SHERRY (Pleasant Valley Wine Co., Hammondsport, N.Y.), $1.99.

BERINGER NAPA VALLEY PALE DRY SHERRY (California) (Beringer Bros., Inc., St. Helena, Calif.), $2.15.

LOUIS M. MARTINI CALIFORNIA COCKTAIL SHERRY (Louis M. Martini, St. Helena, Calif.), $2.15.

SANDEMAN COCKTAIL SHERRY FINO (W. A. Taylor & Co., N.Y.C.), $3.69. Spanish.

PEDRO DOMECQ LA INA COCKTAIL SHERRY (Canada Dry Corp., N.Y.C.), $4. Spanish.

HARVEY'S EXTRA DRY BRISTOL FINO SHERRY (Heublein, Inc.), $6.95 ($6.79 for 25 oz.). Spanish.

ACCEPTABLE—Fair

MEIER'S NO. 11 PALE DRY COCKTAIL OHIO STATE SHERRY (Meier's Wine Cellars, Inc., Silverton, Ohio), $1.99.

SWEET SHERRIES

ACCEPTABLE—Good

CRESTA BLANCA CALIFORNIA SHERRY (Cresta Blanca), $1.98.

GREAT WESTERN NEW YORK STATE CREAM SHERRY (Pleasant Valley Wine Co.), $1.99.

PEDRO DOMECQ CELEBRATION CREAM SHERRY (Canada Dry Corp.), $4.85. Spanish.

ACCEPTABLE—Fair-to-Good

PETRI CRYSTAL CALIFORNIA PURE CREAM SHERRY (Petri Wineries), 96¢ ($1.20 a quart).

COAST TO COAST CALIFORNIA CREAM SHERRY (A&P), 97¢.

GALLO CREAM SHERRY OF CALIFORNIA (Gallo Vineyards), $1 ($1.25 a quart).

ROMA RESERVE CALIFORNIA CREAM SHERRY (Roma Wine Co.), $1.03 ($1.29 a quart).

ITALIAN SWISS COLONY GOLD MEDAL RESERVE CALIFORNIA CREAM SHERRY (Italian Swiss Colony), $1.10.

BRISTOL CLUB AMERICAN TRIPLE CREAM SHERRY (Gimbel Bros.), $1.39.

PAUL MASSON CALIFORNIA GOLDEN CREAM SHERRY (Paul Masson Vineyards), $1.80.

GOLD SEAL NEW YORK STATE CREAM SHERRY (Gold Seal Vineyards, Inc.), $1.85.

THE CHRISTIAN BROTHERS PURE CALIFORNIA CREAM SHERRY (The Christian Bros.), $1.90.

BERINGER NAPA VALLEY PRIVATE STOCK CALIFORNIA SHERRY (Beringer Bros., Inc.), $1.94.

TAYLOR NEW YORK STATE CREAM SHERRY (The Taylor Wine Co., Inc.), $1.94.

WIDMER GOLDEN CREAM NEW YORK STATE SHERRY (Widmer's Wine Cellars, Inc.), $1.95.

WIDMER'S NEW YORK STATE SHERRY—SPECIAL SELECTION (Widmer's Wine Cellars, Inc.), $2.25.

CRESTA BLANCA TRIPLE CREAM CALIFORNIA SHERRY (Cresta Blanca Vineyards), $2.59.

PAUL MASSON RARITY CALIFORNIA RARE CREAM SHERRY (Paul Masson Vineyards), $3.

LOUIS M. MARTINI CALIFORNIA CREAM SHERRY (Louis M. Martini), $3.15.

MEIER'S NO. 44 AMERICAN CREAM SHERRY (Meier's Wine Cellars, Inc.), $3.19.

YORK HOUSE ESTRELLA CREAM SHERRY (R. H. Macy & Co., Inc.), $3.57 ($3.49 for 25 oz.). Spanish.

SANDEMAN FINE RICH CREAM SHERRY (W. A. Taylor & Co.), $3.69. Spanish.

CYRIL'S OWN CREAM SHERRY—ST. EDMUNDS HALL (Private-label brand for Sherry-Lehmann, Inc., N.Y.C.), $4.95. Spanish.

WILLIAMS & HUMBERT CANASTA CREAM SHERRY (Julius Wile Sons & Co., Inc.), $4.98. Spanish.

SANDEMAN ARMADA CREAM OLOROSO SHERRY (W. A. Taylor & Co.), $6.99. Spanish.

HARVEY'S BRISTOL CREAM SHERRY (Heublein, Inc.), $7.32 ($7.15 for 25 oz.). Spanish.

DUFF GORDON CREAM SHERRY (Munson G. Shaw Co.), $7.46 ($7.29 for 25 oz.). Spanish.

ACCEPTABLE—Fair

RED STAR PRIVATE STOCK CALIFORNIA CREAM SHERRY (R. H. Macy & Co., Inc.), $1.10.

ALMADEN CALIFORNIA SOLERA CREAM SHERRY (Almadén Vineyards), $1.92.

BV CALIFORNIA CREAM SHERRY (Beaulieu Vineyard), $1.99.

~~~~~~~~~~~~~~~~~~~~~~~~~~~~~~~~~~~~~~

Chapter 8

FLAVORED WINES

An aperitif has no single definition. It might be described as a mildly alcoholic drink (usually a rather ordinary fortified wine—15 per cent to 20 per cent alcohol—plus assorted flavorings) that, taken before a meal, is designed to put an edge on one's appetite. And, indeed, many of the dry aperitifs do have the sort of taste—sharp, tangy—that seems to rev up the digestive juices. But what about the numerous sweet aperitifs available? Doesn't their taste—not to mention their sugar content—cloy instead of stimulate? One would think so, but the popularity of some of them, particularly in France, suggests otherwise. The fact is, a *small* amount of alcohol in almost any kind of predinner beverage is likely to make you feel a little hungry.

Among the best-known aperitifs are dry and sweet vermouths. (Dry sherry is certainly an aperitif, but it was considered separately—see Chapter 7.) Others include bitters (such as Italy's Campari and Fernet Branca) and brand-name "cocktail wines" (such as Dubonnet and Lillet). CU's expert wine tasters did not test bitters, but they did test, in three separate projects, dry vermouths, sweet vermouths, and brand-name cocktail wines. As usual, in making their tests, they sipped from anonymous, coded samples. First they explored the character and quality of each brand's flavor and aroma; then they scored each brand for overall quality. Some significant—possibly money-saving—findings emerged from their evaluations of the thirty-six flavored wines tasted.

VERMOUTHS, DRY AND SWEET

Vermouths date from the eighteenth century, when the sweet variety was developed in Italy and the dry in France. Today sweet vermouths are still known as "Italian" and dry as "French," but producers in many other countries now make vermouth. And all of them—even in France and Italy—make both sweet and dry versions. In Italy sweet vermouth is used more commonly as a dessert wine than as an aperitif. In America it turns up most often as an ingredient of the manhattan cocktail—just as dry vermouth figures here mainly as a component of the dry martini. But widely prevalent though martinis and manhattans are, all vermouth—domestic and imported, sweet and dry—accounts for only about 3 per cent of this country's total wine sales. Vermouth-on-the rocks, though a fashionable drink in some quarters, has not changed matters.

Vermouth-making, though reasonably complicated, has become pretty much an assembly-line affair. Some European producers may take up to four years for the process, but they are the exceptions. The base of vermouth is almost always an undistinguished wine, generally white (or, in California, dry sherry), to which is added sugar syrup, or *mistelle* (unfermented grape juice stabilized with brandy). Then come the flavorings, chosen—often according to a "secret formula"—from an all but endless number of herbs, roots, barks, leaves, seeds, peels, and flowers. These are steeped in alcohol, which is eventually combined with the wine. The wry taste of wormwood blossoms (the more toxic leaves, used to make absinthe, are unlawful) will be, or should be, present in the final mixture—the name "vermouth" comes from *Wermut,* the German word for "wormwood." So, too, will the taste of some of the following: allspice, coriander seeds, cinnamon, rhubarb, nutmeg, cinchona bark, saffron, cloves, hysop, marjoram, rose petals, angelica root, bitter orange peel, blessed thistle, camomile, gentian, century, quinine, anise, vanilla (traces of the last three items are evident in virtually all sweet vermouths), etc., etc. One maker asserts that 50 herbs and spices go into his product.

The findings

You might think that, with such an arsenal of infusions, the one thing you'd be sure to get in any brand of dry or sweet vermouth was individuality. Apparently, however, the producers have taken pains to have their little pinches of this, that, and the other add up to bland conformity. CU's tasters found very little in most cases to distinguish domestics from imports or one brand from another.

The panelists sampled both the dry and the sweet vermouths of five domestic producers and seven Italian or French producers. Label claims of *dry, very dry,* and even *extra dry,* notwithstanding, they judged all the dry vermouths to be somewhere between dry and intermediate, with the domestic G&D Dry somewhat sweeter than the others. And among the sweet vermouths all but the rather dry Christian Brothers Sweet were found to cluster around a mid-point between dryness and sweetness.

Nevertheless, in both categories the panelists were able to make overall quality distinctions. A single dry vermouth, the French J. Boissiere Vermouth de Chambery, was rated Good. Seven drys were rated Fair-to-Good; and four were rated only Fair, among them the relatively expensive and well-known Italian brand Martini & Rossi. At $2.64 the equivalent fifth, top-rated Boissiere cost about the same as Martini & Rossi and only a little more than Noilly Prat, which was rated Fair-to-Good. But if you want to stretch your pennies—and our consultants see no reason why you shouldn't, especially if you use dry vermouth chiefly for martinis—consider the domestic brands Lejon and Tribuno. Neither scored as high as the Boissiere but each would save you more than a dollar a fifth.

As for the sweet vermouths, two of them were rated Good: the $1.48-a-fifth Tribuno and Martini & Rossi Vino, which cost $2.52 for an equivalent fifth. Each of these two brands scored better in its sweet version than it did in its dry. On the other hand, J. Boissiere Sweet Chambery scored worse than its dry stablemate, rating only Fair-to-Good. At a dollar less than the other top-rated brand, Tribuno Sweet seems a wise buy.

Ratings of Vermouths

Within types, listed by groups in order of estimated overall quality, based on judgments of CU's expert taste panel, and within groups by increasing price. Prices (per fifth) are recommended retail for New York State or the cost equivalent of a fifth for other bottle sizes (actual price and size are then shown parenthetically); prices may differ in other states, but their relationship among brands should be similar.

DRY VERMOUTHS

ACCEPTABLE—Good

J. BOISSIERE VERMOUTH DE CHAMBERY (Munson G. Shaw Co., N.Y.C.), $2.64 ($3.09 for 30 oz.). French.

ACCEPTABLE—Fair-to-Good

TRIBUNO DRY VERMOUTH ("21" Brands, Inc., N.Y.C.), $1.48.

LEJON EXTRA DRY VERMOUTH (Lejon Champagne Cellars, San Francisco), $1.55.

CORA VERY DRY VERMOUTH (Cora Vermouth Import Co., Chicago), $1.73 ($2.29 for 33.8 oz.). Italian.

STOCK DRY VERMOUTH (Schenley Import Co., N.Y.C.), $1.80 ($2.11 for 30 oz.). Italian.

GANCIA DRY VERMOUTH (Garneau Co., N.Y.C.), $1.99. Italian.

NOILLY PRAT EXTRA DRY VERMOUTH (Browne-Vintners Co., N.Y.C.), $2.34 ($2.75 for 30 oz.). French.

CINZANO EXTRA DRY VERMOUTH (Schieffelin & Co., N.Y.C.), $2.65. French.

ACCEPTABLE—Fair

G&D DRY VERMOUTH (Gambarelli & Davitto, Newark, N.J.), $1.41 ($1.65 for 30 oz.). Judged somewhat sweeter than the other brands.

TAYLOR EXTRA DRY VERMOUTH (The Taylor Wine Co., Inc., Hammondsport, N.Y.), $1.50.

THE CHRISTIAN BROTHERS STARLIGHT DRY VERMOUTH (The Christian Bros., Napa, Calif.), $1.75.

MARTINI & ROSSI VERMOUTH (Renfield Importers Ltd., Union, N.J.), $2.52 ($2.95 for 30 oz.). Italian.

SWEET VERMOUTHS

ACCEPTABLE—Good

TRIBUNO SWEET VERMOUTH ("21" Brands, Inc.), $1.48.

MARTINI & ROSSI VINO VERMOUTH (Renfield Importers Ltd.), $2.52 ($2.95 for 30 oz.). Italian.

ACCEPTABLE—Fair-to-Good

G&D SWEET VERMOUTH (Gambarelli & Davitto), $1.41 ($1.65 for 30 oz.).

LEJON SWEET VERMOUTH (Lejon Champagne Cellars), $1.55.

CORA VERMOUTH (Cora Vermouth Import Co.), $1.73 ($2.29 for 33.8 oz.). Italian.

THE CHRISTIAN BROTHERS SWEET VERMOUTH (The Christian Bros.), $1.75.

STOCK ITALIAN VERMOUTH (Schenley Import Co.), $1.80 ($2.11 for 30 oz.). Italian.

GANCIA VERMOUTH (Garneau Co.), $1.99. Italian.

NOILLY PRAT ITALIAN SWEET VERMOUTH (Browne-Vintners Co.), $2.34 ($2.75 for 30 oz.). Italian.

J. BOISSIERE SWEET CHAMBERY VERMOUTH (Munson G. Shaw Co.), $2.64 ($3.09 for 30 oz.). French.

CINZANO ITALIAN SWEET VERMOUTH (Schieffelin & Co.), $2.65. Italian.

ACCEPTABLE—Fair

TAYLOR SWEET VERMOUTH (The Taylor Wine Co., Inc.), $1.50.

BRAND-NAME COCKTAIL WINES

Some of these secret-recipe potions are not only *like* vermouths— if you read their labels closely, you will discover that some *are* vermouths. All were judged sweeter, however, than any regular vermouth tested, falling between intermediate and sweet on our tasters' scale. Even Dubonnet Blonde, which proclaims itself "the world's driest drink," was not an exception to this finding. The French, who more or less invented the cocktail wine, apparently have a sweet tooth that won't let up even during the cocktail hour. All the tested brands were found to be a composite (balanced or

"Pop" Wines

In recent years a whole new category of flavored grape and other natural fruit wines has developed. Ranging in alcoholic content from 9 per cent to 12 per cent, these wines have become beverages more like soft drinks, to be drunk casually, with or without food, rather than table wines to be savored seriously. Their primary quality is refreshment, with flavors that run from apple and cranberry to orange, pineapple, and papaya. Their names are as exotic as their flavors: Boone's Farm Apple, Zapple, Annie Green Springs, Bali Hai, Key Largo, Spañada, Ripple, and a trio named I, Love, and You. They are bottled in containers of all sizes—some even in 12-ounce soda-type bottles—and should be well chilled for serving. They cost roughly $1 to $1.25 a fifth; in larger sizes, the cost per ounce is less. If they appeal to you, keep in mind that you're drinking an alcoholic beverage, not soda pop.

otherwise—see comments on each in the Ratings) of spicy, floral, and fruity aromas and flavors.

The results

Judging proprietary aperitifs was not made easier by the fact that each of them is blended to be unique. How do you compare one-of-a-kinds? Our panelists did somehow manage to arrive at a few decisions concerning them, but they are decisions you are urged to forget if you find one or another particularly appealing to your taste.

None of the brands was considered outstandingly good or bad. Lady Widmer Golden Cocktail and the two Lillet wines (from France) were judged to be a bit better than the other aperitifs in the test. Of the four brand-pairs tested, Lady Widmer Golden was rated above Lady Widmer Silver, and the fruity St. Raphaël Red was thought superior in flavor and aroma to its more floral sibling, St. Raphaël Golden. On the other hand, the experts found little difference between the two high-rated Lillets and not much between the two Dubonnets. Probably the sensible thing for you to do, if you're interested in becoming acquainted with cocktail wines, is to start off with the less expensive brands. If you like one of them, stay with it. If you don't, try Lady Widmer Golden, at $1.75. Then, if it doesn't please you either, you might as well try one or the other of the Lillet pair. Note, though: they're $3.99 a fifth. You can pick up a good dry sherry at a much lower price than that, if your tastes tend in that direction.

CU's consultants recommend that you serve vermouth or cocktail wine in an 8-ounce stemmed tulip-shaped glass filled halfway, at most—unless you're pouring it over ice, in which case an old-fashioned glass is indicated. You may prefer your cocktail wine at room temperature; the experts preferred theirs chilled.

Ratings of Cocktail Wines

Listed by groups in order of estimated overall quality, based on judgments of CU's expert taste panel, and within groups by increasing price. Prices (per fifth) are recommended retail for New York State or the cost equivalent of a fifth for other bottle sizes (actual price and size are then shown parenthetically); prices may differ in other states, but their relationship among brands should be similar.

ACCEPTABLE—Good

LADY WIDMER NEW YORK STATE GOLDEN COCKTAIL APERITIF WINE (Widmer's Wine Cellars, Inc., Naples, N.Y.), $1.75. Moderate floral-fruity flavor character.

LILLET GOLD LABEL (Dreyfus, Ashby & Co., N.Y.C.), $3.99. Moderate spicy-fruity flavor character. French.

LILLET WHITE LABEL (Dreyfus, Ashby & Co.), $3.99. Moderate spicy-fruity flavor character. French.

ACCEPTABLE—Fair-to-Good

ROMA ROCKET (Roma Wine Co., Fresno, Calif.), $1. Sweet, strong flavor character with faint spicy-floral tones. (Not distributed in New York State.)

THUNDERBIRD APERITIF WINE (Gallo Vineyards, Modesto, Calif.), $1. Sweet, moderate fruity flavor character with faint spicy-floral tones.

LADY WIDMER NEW YORK STATE SILVER COCKTAIL APERITIF WINE (Widmer's Wine Cellars, Inc.), $1.75. Moderate, blended flavor character.

POSITANO (Frederick Wildman & Sons, N.Y.C.), $2.54 ($2.99 for 30 oz.). Moderate spicy flavor character. French.

ST. RAPHAEL GOLDEN APERITIF WINE (Renfield Importers, Ltd., Union, N.J.), $3.30. Sweet, strong, blended flavor character. French.

ST. RAPHAEL RED APERITIF WINE (Renfield Importers, Ltd.), $3.30. Sweet, strong, full-bodied, moderately fruity-floral flavor character. French.

BYRRH (Heublein, Inc., Hartford, Conn.), $3.72 ($3.49 for 24 oz.). Sweet, strong, blended flavor character. French.

DUBONNET BLONDE EXTRA DRY WHITE WINE APERITIF (Dubonnet Co., Fresno, Calif.), $3.99. Moderate floral flavor character with faint spicy-fruity tones.

DUBONNET (Dubonnet Co.), $3.99. Sweet, moderate blended flavor character.

SPIRITS

~~~~~~~~~~~~~~~~~~~~~~~~~~~~~~~~~~~

Chapter 9

A FEW WORDS
ON SPIRITS

Long before the birth of Christ men were distilling scents and water—making drinking water from sea water, for example. But, as far as we know, it wasn't until the tenth century A.D. that alcohol was distilled, by the Arabs. The word "alcohol," in fact, comes from the Arabic *al-koh'l*. Kohl, however, is not some middle-eastern version of Scotch but a distillate that was, and still is, used as an eye shadow.

THE PROCESS OF DISTILLATION

Because alcohol has a lower boiling point than water, the recipe for distilling a fermented mixture is, basically, to boil it until the alcohol rises as a vapor and then to trap that vapor and let it cool back into a liquid. This liquid, being more highly alcoholic than the wine or mash from which it was derived, was said to contain the parent mixture's soul or spirit—hence the term "spirits."

Distilled spirits vary widely. Some, such as whiskey, brandy, and rum, show a broad range of flavor and character. Gin, on the other hand, has a narrow range, and domestic vodka, by law, has scarcely any range at all. A somewhat longer look at the distillation process will help to explain why these differences and lack of differences exist. There are two distinct types of distilling apparatus in use today—the pot still and the patent, or column, still.

The Meaning of Proof

"Proof" is the standard measure of the alcohol content of spirits. In the United States and Canada this measure is exactly twice the percentage of alcohol that a given spirit contains. Thus, pure alcohol (possible only under laboratory conditions) would be 200 proof, whereas a spirit that is half alcohol is 100 proof.

Hundred-proof liquor is known as "proof spirit" because of a crude but serviceable technique by which some early distillers determined drinking strength. They mixed a sample of the spirit with gunpowder and tried to light it. If the mixture would not ignite, the distillate was considered too weak; if an overly bright flare leaped up, the spirit was too potent. A steady blue flame denoted a distillate of proper strength for drinking; spirits yielding such a flame were said to have been "proved."

When laboratory techniques came to be applied, it turned out that such "proof spirits" were 50 per cent alcohol, more or less. This figure was accordingly designated 100 proof in the arbitrary standard by which proof is reckoned in the United States. (Different, but equally arbitrary, systems are used in some other countries.)

An awareness of proof is important to consumers, not only because of its obvious effect on the intoxicating quality of a drink, but also because of its effect on liquor prices. A large fraction of the cost of liquor represents the U.S. Internal Revenue tax and corresponding state taxes. These taxes are levied in direct proportion to proof. In New York State, for example, which has a rather typical alcohol tax, the price of a 100-proof fifth of liquor includes about $2.77 in Federal and state taxes, but an 80-proof fifth pays only $2.33. As a conscientious buyer, you would normally be alert to the differences in bottle size—a quart instead of a fifth, for example—but you might well assume that competing bottles lined up on a shelf had the same proof. Or expect a standard proof on a brand you buy regularly. However, a distiller can, at his discretion, cut back on proof without making a corresponding cut in his price, thus concealing what amounts to a price increase.

The pot still

A fairly uncomplicated distilling apparatus is the primitive pot still, which is relied on to this day in the Cognac district of France, in the highlands of Scotland, and in certain militantly unmechanized areas of Kentucky and Tennessee. It consists, typically, of a large copper pot with a broad, rounded bottom and a long, tapered neck, connected to a worm condenser—a jacketed spiral of copper tubing. As the mixture in the pot is heated, the vapors rise into the tubing, where, thanks to the cooling water circulating in the jacket, they condense. The final section of the still, the receiver, receives the condensation, or distillate, from the condenser.

The pot distilling of some liquors may involve a second or even a third distillation to achieve the desired quality or alcoholic level of the distillate. In the making of brandy, the mixture that goes into the pot is a wine or the liquid from a fermented fruit mash. The making of whiskey, gin, or vodka calls for the liquid from a fermented grain mash, and the making of rum requires the liquid from a fermented sugar-cane mash. Whatever the mixture, it will contain, in addition to ethyl alcohol and water, small quantities of fusel oils (higher-boiling alcohols), acids, esters, aldehydes, and other volatile substances, all of which differ in the temperature at which they vaporize.

Once the fire is lighted under the pot, the water turned on in the condenser, and the distilling started, the composition of what comes over into the receiver can be controlled by adjusting the temperature of the mash in the pot. The hotter the pot becomes, the more water evaporates and the lower the alcoholic level (called "proof"—see box for explanation) of the distillate. Distilling out at or above 190 proof gives "neutral spirits" or, if a fermented grain mash has been used, "grain neutral spirits."* Either way, the

---

* As of July 1, 1972, a new term, "grain spirits," has been used to designate grain neutral spirits that have been stored in oak containers. Such storage may not be called "aging," but producers are now able to advertise that their "grain spirits" have been "stored four years in oak containers" and thus are now able to indicate that the spirits are more than merely "neutral."

liquid is colorless with little or no taste or odor other than that of alcohol. Dilute grain neutral spirits with water, and, to all intents and purposes, you will have vodka. Dilute them with water and then infuse them with certain aromatic botanicals, and you'll have gin. Or you can use them as a base for a cordial or mix them with a whiskey to produce a spirit blend.

The lower the proof, the less pure the alcohol. However, "purity" in this context is a descriptive, not a judgmental term, referring to concentration of alcohol in the solution, for it is the minute traces of impurities, or "congeners," in a liquor—the fusel oils, acids, and so on—that distinguish its own special flavor and aroma. Typically, light-bodied rums and Canadian whiskies are distilled at roughly 180 proof, whereas Bourbon, malt Scotch whiskies, and full-bodied rums are distilled at 160 proof or below.

The patent still

The patent, or column, still was invented early in the last century and is used today throughout the world in the production of whiskey and most other distilled spirits. Unlike pot distillation, which is a batch process, distillation by patent still is a continuous operation. It produces a distillate of uniform character with a minimum of labor.

In the patent still the mixture to be distilled trickles down a series of plates, or baffles, within the column, to be met by a stream of vapor rising from the bottom of the column. The outcome of the meeting is an almost instantaneous stripping of the more volatile constituents with little of the mixture having been overheated for any length of time. The mixture in a pot still, on the contrary, remains heated for as long as the process goes on. The patent still, as a result, affords much more precise control over the constituency of the spirit being produced.

AGING AND BLENDING

Congeners—the flavor ingredients—can also be modified by aging.

Distilled spirits, if aged at all, are aged in wood casks. Unlike table wines, they do not age in the bottle. Aging in wood is important to whiskies, brandies, and most rums, for it affects the congeners in them so that their originally harsh taste becomes smoother and mellower. Aging may also deepen the color of a liquor. (In many products, however, most of the coloring is added separately by the producer.)

With so much of the distilling process in his own hands rather than in nature's, the distiller clearly has far more influence over his product than the maker of an unblended table wine has over his. In a bad year there is little a vintner can do to avoid producing mediocre table wine, but splendid brandies can be, and are, made from rather poor wines. Indeed the distiller need not ever have a "bad" year. He can use his distilling, aging, and blending techniques to even out natural variations and maintain a uniform product for as long as he likes. Therefore, a reader who arrives at his own brand selections through using CU's Ratings and Recommendations of spirits may well remain satisfied with his choices—unless his tastes change, or the producer of "his" brand deliberately changes the nature of the liquor.

CU'S TESTS OF SPIRITS

For most liquor types discussed in this book, brand-name buying advice is based on carefully controlled taste tests. Tested spirits included whiskies, gins, vodkas, light rums, and grape brandies (Cognacs and others) of France and the United States. CU also taste-tested premixed cocktails and cocktail mixes, and Chapter 15 summarizes our findings on these aids to faster (but not necessarily better) mixed drinks.

Because they account for only a very small fraction of spirits sales in the United States, CU did *not* test imported grape brandies other than French or any brandies made from fruits other than the grape, nor did we sample dark rums, tequila, other flavored neutral spirits such as akvavit, or cordials. Brand-buying advice for those products is based on our consultants' Recommendations, taking into account brand availability. (In some instances, only one or two brands—not necessarily the ones our consultants would choose —have any significant distribution.)

The results of most of our liquor taste-tests are reported here as Ratings, with appropriate indications of relative quality and other differences. Within some product categories, however, no reliable quality variations were discerned, and straight listings of the brands in question are therefore provided. These are arranged by cost, starting with the least expensive, and alphabetically at the same cost.

For our liquor-tasting projects CU assembled taste panels with "educated palates," just as we did for our tests of wines. Each panel was made up of four to six expert tasters—professionals and distinguished amateurs who had acquired, from wide experience in the tasting of spirits, a knowledge of what to look for, and who had, at the same time, the ability to express their judgments with some precision.

All tastings were "blind"—the products were identified only by code numbers and included duplicate, but differently coded, samples of each brand. Only a few samples were tasted at one time because the high alcoholic content of spirits tends to numb the taste buds and olfactory senses. In most cases the taster sniffed and mouthed, without swallowing.

Every brand was tasted at least twice by each taster, each time at a different tasting session. The order of tasting of the samples in any one group was controlled so that specimens of each sample would be tasted early in one sitting and late in another and in conjunction with different samples each time. Besides making over-all quality judgments, the tasters evaluated such specific characteristics as aroma, flavor, and body.

Typically, the procedure went like this: First each expert sniffed the sample before him to evaluate its aroma. Then he diluted a portion with distilled water, took a sip and rolled it around in his mouth to check its flavor. Then he spat out the sip and checked the aftertaste, an important characteristic. Finally, the panelist rinsed his mouth with water before moving on to the next sample.

Aroma and flavor interact, though in a complex and unpredictable way, sometimes in harmony, sometimes at odds. These characteristics were assessed for both strength and quality, which are not equivalent. A liquor's aroma, for example, can be at once weak in strength and high in quality. Evaluations were also made, where appropriate, of harshness or smoothness on the palate and of the balance between aroma, flavor, and palate impression.

As you read the results of these tastings, keep in mind that testing alcoholic beverages by sensory means can be a tricky business. The testers are, after all, human beings, with personal likes and dislikes. Your own tastes may agree with those of our panelists, but, then again, they may not. At times the tasters did not agree among themselves (demonstrating one of the reasons we used panels of four to six).

SHOPPING FOR SPIRITS

The best place to buy wines is not always the best place to buy spirits. In Chapter 1 we gave you some reasons why you might want to (or have to) rely on a knowledgeable wine merchant. In the uncertain world of wines, it is reassuring to get his advice on such matters as vintages, unknown vineyards, shippers, and even what wine to serve with what food.

The world of spirits, on the other hand, is a much more certain world. For one thing, distilled spirits, once bottled, do not change appreciably, so that delicate and careful handling is not as important. Secondly, most spirits are designed to be uniform from bottle to bottle and year to year, unless the producer alters his formula (which is not often). Thus, Brand X in one store can be expected to match Brand X in any other store. Shopping for widely distributed name brands, then, comes down pretty much to a matter of price. Comparison shopping in your particular locality is the only way to tell if you can save, and how much. If you're in a "control" state (see pages 17-18), of course, no such shopping is possible.

When you look beyond the name brands, you'll find the choice of store does make some difference. Many stores have their own "house" brands—lower-priced, private-labeled stock that is bottled just for them (or for a group of stores). Some of CU's taste tests included private-label brands, and often they came out quite creditably. Unless you value the status symbolism of name labels, it will generally pay you (in money terms) to try private brands. The label must characterize the type of spirit and give its proof, so if the flavor suits you, buy it and serve it.

Prices

The prices of distilled spirits in this book, unless otherwise noted, are the manufacturer's suggested retail prices in New York State as of June 1, 1972. They are current standard prices for the size bottle indicated and do not reflect "sale" prices, which may be in effect for short periods (watch for them). In other states, prices may vary depending on local regulations and/or distributors' policies; however, there is not much variation in the price relationships among the brands. Where differences in proof and age affect prices, these are pointed up in the text describing the liquor types involved.

~~~~~~

Chapter 10

WHISKIES

Whiskey* is the most popular distilled spirit in the United States by a wide margin. A person without much experience in buying and serving whiskey is apt to find himself bewildered by the diversity of types and brands available, as well as by often conflicting advice on what to buy. Even a regular whiskey drinker can be forgiven some confusion. The results of CU's blind taste tests of whiskies may offer some comfort in the way of guidelines to both novices and initiates.

WHISKIES IN GENERAL

All whiskies are distilled from fermented grain mashes, but both the kinds of grain and the way they are converted from raw cereal to particular bottled spirits vary considerably from place to place, and the product varies accordingly. Four countries—the United States, Canada, Scotland, and Ireland—are the major manufacturers of whiskey. The United States produces mainly Bourbon and spirit blends, commonly but incorrectly referred to as "rye," with corn usually the dominant grain in both products. (Few brands of straight rye or blended straight rye are sold today.) The basic grain flavor in Scotch and Irish whiskey is barley; in Canadian whiskey, corn, rye, and wheat are all used in the mash.

---

* Though whiskey is traditionally spelled "whisky" in referring to Scotch and Canadian types, its spelling is quite arbitrary in American usage. For the sake of uniformity, it will be used with the "e" throughout this book.

Whatever the dominant grain, it is mixed with malt, which is mostly sprouted (malted) barley. The starches in the grain will not ferment unless malt is added to initiate the conversion into fermentable sugars; the sugars, in turn, are turned into carbon dioxide and alcohol by the addition of yeasts not unlike those used in baking. The raw whiskey distilled from the mash is barreled and aged.

After aging, whiskies are diluted to the desired proof with water and bottled, either "straight" (unblended) or in blends. Blending straight whiskies together results in a product that is called, logically enough, a blend of straight whiskies. Blending whiskey with neutral spirits (unflavored, unaged grain alcohol) produces what is called a spirit blend. Recent changes in Federal regulations have freed producers from some of the restrictions hitherto placed on production methods, and in consequence one newly authorized type of whiskey has appeared on the market (see the comments on Light Whiskey, facing page).

How they differ

As explained in the preceding chapter, the main thing that makes one whiskey different from another (and from neutral spirits) is its congeners, small amounts of various substances that impart flavor and aroma. A whiskey relatively rich in congeners will generally have a strong bouquet and a full flavor and body; one low in congeners, a weak bouquet and a light body. The total amounts and identities of the congeners in a given bottle of whiskey will depend mainly on the grain used, the proof at which the whiskey was distilled, the number of years aged, the kind of barrels used for the aging, and the amount, if any, of grain neutral spirits that were added.

Highest in congeners—and fullest in body—are the Bourbons. Next in line are unblended single-malt Scotches, then Irish whiskies, then the blended Scotches, which vary in body but are now generally on the light side. Lightest of all are the Canadian whiskies, the new Light Whiskies, and the spirit blends, the former two mainly because of the process used to distill them, the latter mainly because they are blends of straight whiskeys with congener-free grain neutral spirits.

To a point, longer aging of a given whiskey will make it perceptibly smoother; nevertheless one should not be hypnotized by age statements on the labels. For one thing, age is no guarantee of quality; a poor whiskey will improve with aging but is not likely to become a superior whiskey, no matter how many years appear on the label. For another, after a certain number of years of aging, whiskey reaches a point of diminishing returns, beyond which the differences created by additional aging become almost imperceptible. And finally, different types of whiskey age at different rates, so that four years of aging for one type may be the equivalent of six for another.

Perhaps the most remarkable change in the drinking preferences of Americans over the last decade or so has been a consistent trend toward mildness—real or imagined lightness in body, flavor, aroma, and color. To cash in on this "revolution," as people in the industry have called it, the distillers have brought to market a number of new and ever-milder brands. And the ads for many of the old brands are rigged to give the consumer the idea that these established standbys are mild, too. Indeed, it is not beyond the realm of possibility that subtle shifts actually have been made in the formulations of each type.

One very specific result of this change in drinking preferences was Federal authorization of Light Whiskey, which was sold for the first time on July 1, 1972. American producers can now distill whiskey between 160 and 190 proof and age it in used barrels, which should result in a whiskey with a flavor milder than the typical American blends. The distillers also have more freedom in the use of this new whiskey in blends and are not required to include on their labels the exact composition of the blend. No Light Whiskey was included in CU's tests, which were completed before it was available. Readers who would like to taste-test it for themselves should try it in the triangle test (page 11) against one of their favorite Canadian whiskies or American spirit blends.

CU's tests

CU's panel tasted 112 brands of Scotch, Irish, Canadian, Bourbon, and spirit blends. Widely sold brands were included in the test as well as comparative unknowns with some special appeal, such as price or unique flavor.

The overall quality of each sample was evaluated according to a scale of Excellent, Very Good, Good, Fair, and Poor. The Ratings as a whole were based on the average of the experts' judgments of overall quality. But to help readers choose a brand to fit their own tastes, the experts recorded as well their impressions of three characteristics—bouquet, flavor, and body. Where they wished, the experts made additional comments, also included in the Ratings.

General conclusions

The positiveness of the experts' judgment as to quality varied with the type of whiskey; what they could not tell proved as interesting as what they could. With the Scotch and Irish whiskies and the Bourbons, they were moderately sure of themselves; by and large their evaluations were fairly consistent. Even so, the differences in quality were admittedly pretty fine. Not so fine as the quality differences in the Canadian whiskies and U.S. spirit blends, however. The experts not only couldn't tell the brands apart but were unable to distinguish between the two types! It is hard to avoid the conclusion that differences among whiskies are not nearly as great as most people believe—certainly a lot less than the ads claim.

Most of the prices in the Ratings are those recommended by the manufacturer in New York State. A few of the brands aren't sold there, however, and for these the prices given are those in California or New Jersey, as noted. The prices given are current (as of June 1, 1972); proofs and other pertinent information were verified as well, and discovered changes were made in the Ratings. In the judgment of CU's consultants, such changes usually do not alter the quality of the products, and the Ratings should remain applicable.

SCOTCH AND IRISH WHISKIES

Whiskey was first produced some nine centuries ago by a Gaelic tribe using malted barley. (The word "whiskey" is derived from the Gaelic for "water of life.") It is not known whether this tribe was composed of Scots or Irishmen, though present-day Scots and Irish harbor strong, if divergent, views on the matter. In any event, both Scotland and Ireland use malted barley to this day in making their whiskies.

Scotch whiskies

Most Scotch whiskies sold in the United States are blends of grain whiskies and malt whiskies. It is the latter, made entirely from malted, or sprouted, barley, that gives Scotch its characteristic smoky, peaty flavor. As it dries in a kiln heated by a smoldering peat fire, the malt becomes impregnated by the acrid peat smoke rising through the screenlike floor, and the flavor it thus acquires is carried into the finished whiskey. Distilled today as it was in the past—in pot stills at a rather low proof (about 140)—malt whiskey is quite full-bodied, to say the least, with a pungency that few but Scots find to their taste.

Malt whiskies are made in four main regions of Scotland. Those grown in Campbeltown and Islay are generally very heavy and smoky; those from the Highlands (widely considered the best) are lighter and less smoky; and those from the Lowlands are lightest and least smoky of all, and they figure prominently in the blending of the new light-bodied Scotches. Only a few brands of unblended malt Scotch are exported to the United States, though that is a few more than there used to be. One of them—The Glenlivet—was among the Scotches tested.

The continuous column, or patent, still, developed early in the nineteenth century, facilitated production of a light-bodied spirit from grain mash—especially light when distilled, as in current Scottish practice, at a high 180 proof. In the 1850s someone had the imagination to try mixing the lighter, column-still grain whiskies with the rugged pot-still malt whiskies. The fruit of this inspiration was a spirit that could be appreciated outside of Scotland. And appreciated it has been, particularly—and increasingly —in the United States. Scotch accounted for a respectable 12 per cent of all whiskies sold here in 1961—but an astonishing 23 per cent in 1971.

Much of the popularity of this whiskey may be explained by the recent trend to "lightness" in American drinking habits, happily catered to by the Scottish distillers, who in the last few years have sent many new brands of Scotch blended expressly for extra lightness of body. This lightness is largely dependent on the percentage of light grain whiskey in the product. In huge vats the grain whiskey is polygamously "married" with from twenty to fifty different malt whiskies, all of which have been aged in oak casks— ideally, wine-soaked casks made of American oak. But wine-soaked casks aren't always available, and a whiskey stored in a cask that hasn't been wine-soaked will not attain its characteristic color while it ages. No matter: The distiller can simply add caramel coloring to it until it looks like Scotch. Except for rarities, Scotches sold here range from 80 to 86.8 proof.

Irish whiskies

There was a time when Irish whiskey outsold Scotch here, but that was long ago, before the 1850s, when the first Scotch blends took over. Today Irish whiskey sales in this country, although they doubled between 1961 and 1971, amount to only a fraction of 1 per cent of Scotch sales, and the number of Irish brands with more than token distribution in the United States can be counted on the fingers of one hand.

Irish whiskey is usually sold at 86 proof. It tastes vaguely like a light-bodied Scotch, but it has a somewhat stronger, more medicinal flavor. There are real differences, for the two spirits are made differently. The Irish dry their malted barley in peat-fired kilns, as the Scots do, but the Irish kilns have a solid floor, so that the smoke that gives Scotch its smoky flavor doesn't get into Irish malt. Then, too, the Irish blend grain and malt before fermentation, whereas the Scots wait until after aging before blending the grain and malt whiskies. Finally, all Irish whiskey is produced in a pot still and at a much higher proof than Scotch malt whiskies, and it requires more aging than Scotch does—experts say it takes at least seven years for it to reach its peak.

CU's findings

Over two hundred brands and blends of Scotch are exported to the United States, but only about seventy are really promoted, and fewer still are well known. For testing, CU chose thirty-nine Scotches, some of them well known, some obscure. Our selections included high-priced brands, medium-priced brands, and ten brands with lower-than-average prices.

The three brands of Irish whiskey tested were just about the only ones at all widely available in this country. Two of the three come from the Republic of Ireland; Old Bushmill's comes from Northern Ireland.

CU tasters found most of the Scotches to be approximately equal in overall quality, but by no means to have identical characteristics. Panelists discerned differences in flavor, aroma, degree of "Scotchiness," and body. As indicated in the foregoing discussion of blending, Scotches may differ greatly in body—the degree to which a spirit gives a full or thin sensation in the mouth. In fact, the panel considered body to be a sufficiently distinguishing characteristic to warrant grouping the Scotches in the Ratings according to whether they were judged light-bodied, intermediate-bodied, or full-bodied. Bear in mind, however, that although the three degrees of body represent decidedly different taste experiences, CU considers none of the groups inherently better or worse than the others. The question, then, isn't which group tastes best, but which group represents your kind of Scotch.

Among the five full-bodied blends were the only two brands

in the project judged Very Good in overall quality: King's Ransom and Teacher's Highland Cream. Three intermediate Scotches were judged Good: Johnnie Walker Red Label, Vat 69 (but not Vat 69 Gold), and Ambassador 12 Years Old.

Some differences in aroma were discerned by the panelists, but only one blend was singled out as having an aroma of distinctly higher quality, Johnnie Walker Red. This Scotch was commended as well for very good flavor quality, along with King's Ransom. Also cited for good flavor were Vat 69 and Teacher's.

All three Irish whiskies were judged by the panelists to be intermediate in body, as were most of the tested Scotches. The Irish whiskies were all rated Fair-to-Good in overall quality, again like the majority of Scotches tested.

What to buy

Our tasters' comments may help you pick out a Scotch you might like or to avoid one whose character might put you off. If you prefer a light Scotch, for example, The Glenlivet is probably not for you. But The Glenlivet might be worth a try if you want a Scotch with a hefty malt character—and if you have $11 or more to invest in Scotch. At a more moderate price among the full-bodied brands, consider the Very Good Teacher's and King's Ransom. At 94 proof, King's Ransom also delivers more alcohol for your money, if that matters to you.

Johnnie Walker Red is worthy of consideration among Scotches of intermediate body, but don't neglect the possibility that you might be just as happy (and $2 richer) with one of the lower-priced brands (six of them at less than $5.60). All of these lower-priced brands are so-called "bulk imports"—brought into this country at relatively high proof (with a resulting tax saving), brought down to selling proof by adding distilled water, and bottled here. However, they fared no worse in the Ratings than many bottled-in-Scotland Scotches.

A couple of concluding words to the wise: The age of Scotch

whiskies was not much of a guide to anything but price. None of the four twelve-year-old Scotches and none of the eight-year-olds was rated Very Good, and only three (all of them twelve-year-olds) were rated Good. And color doesn't mean much, either. In general, the fuller-bodied blends are likely to be darker than the lighter-bodied. But not always. Johnnie Walker Red and Johnnie Walker Black, for example, seemed to be exactly the same color, though they possessed markedly different characters.

Ratings of Scotch and Irish Whiskies

Listed by types; within types, listed by groups in order of estimated overall quality as judged by CU's expert tasters; within quality groups, listed in order of increasing price. Comments represent a consensus of the tasters' subjective impressions. All whiskies are 86 proof unless otherwise noted. Prices are the recommended retail for a fifth in New York State or California; prices may differ in other states, but the price relationship among brands should be similar.

LIGHT-BODIED SCOTCH WHISKIES

ACCEPTABLE—Fair-to-Good

MacKINTOSH (MacKintosh Importers, Div. of "21" Brands, Inc., N.Y.C.), $5.41. 80 proof. Bottled in U.S.

INTERMEDIATE-BODIED SCOTCH WHISKIES

ACCEPTABLE—Good

JOHNNIE WALKER RED LABEL (Canada Dry Corp., N.Y.C.), $7.85. 86.8 proof. Flavor and aroma judged much better than most.

VAT 69 (Munson G. Shaw Co., N.Y.C.), $7.89. 86.8 proof. Flavor judged better than most; termed "peaty." Aroma, "lusty," "strong."

AMBASSADOR 12 YEARS OLD (Quality Importers, Inc., N.Y.C.), $10.75. Flavor termed "peaty," "big."

ACCEPTABLE—Fair-to-Good

CLAN MacGREGOR (Popper Morson Corp., Jersey City), $5.45. 80 proof. Bottled in U.S.

CRAWFORD'S (Somerset Importers, Ltd., N.Y.C.), $5.45. 80 proof.

Bottled in U.S. Flavor termed "quite peaty." Aroma, "faint" but "smoky."

MUIRHEAD'S (Muirhead Importers, Ltd., N.Y.C.), $5.48. Bottled in U.S. Flavor termed "smooth," "good for type." Aroma, "soft," "light," but "properly Scotchy."

KING GEORGE IV (Munson G. Shaw Co.), $5.49. 80 proof. Bottled in U.S.

KING WILLIAM IV (Renfield Importers, Ltd., Union, N.J.), $5.49. Bottled in U.S.

INVER HOUSE GREEN PLAID (Inver House Distillers, Ltd., Philadelphia), $5.58. 80 proof. Bottled in U.S. Flavor termed "very light."

LAUDER'S (Gooderham & Worts, Ltd., Peoria, Ill.), $5.90. Bottled in U.S. Flavor termed "very light" but "pleasant." Aroma, "low-keyed," "sweetish."

PETER DAWSON "SPECIAL" (Julius Wile Sons & Co., Inc., N.Y.C.), $5.99. Bottled in U.S.

VAT 69 GOLD (Munson G. Shaw Co.), $5.99. Bottled in U.S. Aroma, "rough."

USHER'S GREEN STRIPE (Brown-Forman Distillers Corp., Louisville, Ky.), $6.09. Bottled in U.S.

JOHN BEGG BLUE CAP ("The House of John Begg," N.Y.C.), $6.25, 86.8 proof. Bottled in U.S.

CATTO'S GOLD LABEL (Victor Fischel & Co., Inc., N.Y.C.), $6.44.

"CLUNY" (Scottish & Newcastle Importers Co., N.Y.C.), $6.59. 86.8 proof. Aroma, "smoky," "rather chemical."

OLD SMUGGLER (W. A. Taylor & Co., N.Y.C.), $6.69. Bottled in U.S.

HAIG (Renfield Importers, Ltd.), $6.99. Flavor termed "peaty."

HEDGES & BUTLER ROYAL (Hedges & Butler Imports, Ltd., N.Y.C.), $6.99. Flavor termed "palatable," but "without much character."

MARTIN'S V.V.O. 8 YEARS OLD (McKesson & Robbins, Inc., N.Y.C.), $7.61. 86.8 proof. Flavor and aroma termed "mild."

100 PIPERS (Seagram Distillers Co., N.Y.C.), $7.65.

"BLACK & WHITE" (The Fleischmann Distilling Corp., N.Y.C.), $7.70. 86.8 proof.

CUTTY SARK (The Buckingham Corp., N.Y.C.), $7.71.

LONG JOHN (Long John Importing Co., Div. of Schenley, N.Y.C.), $7.75. Bottled in U.S.

BALLANTINE'S ("21" Brands, Inc., N.Y.C.), $7.79. Flavor termed "light," "medicinal," "good for type."

CHEQUERS (Custom Import House, Ltd., N.Y.C.), $7.80. 86.8 proof. Flavor termed "peaty," "woody."

WHITE HORSE (Browne-Vintners Co., N.Y.C.), $7.83.

DEWAR'S WHITE LABEL (Schenley Import Co., N.Y.C.), $7.85. 86.8 proof.

GRANT'S STAND FAST 8 YEARS OLD (Austin, Nichols & Co., Inc., N.Y.C.), $7.86. Flavor, "light," "peaty."

BELL'S 8 YEARS OLD (Heublein, Inc., Hartford, Conn.), $7.90.

AMBASSADOR DELUXE 8 YEAR (Quality Importers, Inc.), $7.95.

CHIVAS REGAL 12 YEARS OLD (General Wine & Spirits Co., N.Y.C.), $10.45. Flavor termed "peaty," "good for type."

ACCEPTABLE—Fair

J & B RARE (The Paddington Corp., N.Y.C.), $7.85. Flavor judged only fair; termed "too bland," "fading."

FULL-BODIED SCOTCH WHISKIES

ACCEPTABLE—Very Good

TEACHER'S HIGHLAND CREAM (Schieffelin & Co., N.Y.C.), $7.70. Flavor judged better than most. Aroma, "rich," "strong."

KING'S RANSOM "ROUND THE WORLD" (International Brands, Newark, N.J.), $7.99. 94 proof. Flavor judged much better than most. Aroma, "well balanced."

ACCEPTABLE—Good

BELL'S ROYAL VAT 12 YEARS OLD (Heublein, Inc.), $9.55. Flavor termed "strongly peaty." Aroma, "very heavy."

JOHNNIE WALKER BLACK LABEL (Canada Dry Corp.), $10.99. 86.8 proof. Flavor termed "peaty." Aroma, "full," "smoky."

THE GLENLIVET 12 YEARS OLD SINGLE UN-BLENDED MALT WHISKEY (Barton Distillers Import Corp., N.Y.C.), $11.25. 91 proof. Flavor termed "very strong," "malty," "smoky."

IRISH WHISKIES

ACCEPTABLE—Fair-to-Good

OLD BUSHMILL'S (Quality Importers, Inc.), $7.85.

JOHN POWER & SON THREE SWALLOW 7 YEARS OLD (McKesson & Robbins, Inc.), $7.94. Flavor judged only fair; flavor and aroma termed "chemical-medicinal."

JOHN JAMESON & SON 7 YEARS OLD (W. A. Taylor & Co.), $8.39. Bottled in U.S. Aroma, "pungent."

BOURBON

Bourbon is America's own special contribution to the world's whiskey supply—it is also, as of recent date, the most popular whiskey type sold in its homeland. Bourbon takes its name from the county (now in Kentucky) where it was first made, about 1790. In 1964 by congressional resolution, Bourbon was proclaimed a "distinctive product of the United States," and imports were prohibited from using its name. It is, therefore, properly capitalized —Bourbon.

Although most Bourbon is still made in Kentucky, it can be produced in any state. To qualify as a Bourbon, the whiskey must by law be distilled from a mash containing at least 51 per cent corn (but not more than 80 per cent, or it would have to be labeled "corn whiskey"). In general, more corn makes for a lighter body (corn also costs less), and the proportion is typically 65 to 75 per cent. The rest of the mash can be any combination of cereal grains —rye, barley, rice, and others.

Federal regulations require Bourbon to be distilled at not over 160 proof, and it is usually "brought over" at a somewhat lower proof (column stills are almost always used). The resulting whiskies are quite full-bodied, with substantial flavor and aroma. Legally, Bourbon must be aged in new charred-oak barrels for at least two years, but most Bourbon is actually aged four years or more.

Sour mash and sweet mash

Some Bourbons pride themselves on being made by the old "sour mash" process, which may have derived its name from the taste difference it's supposed to impart. If so, CU can only report that our panelists found some sour-mash Bourbons that they considered sweet (and some sweet-mash Bourbons that they did *not* consider sweet). In every Bourbon production, the mash is mixed with water and steamed to start the conversion of starches in the grain to fermentable sugars (a task accomplished by enzymes from the sprouted barley always used in the mash, if only in small quantities). The sugars, in turn, are converted into alcohol by the action of yeast. In the sweet-mash process, fresh yeast goes into the fermenting vessel together with the watered mash, and the mixture is left to ferment for thirty to fifty hours. In the sour-mash process, the watered mash is added to some spent mash from a previous batch (possibly with a little fresh yeast as well); this fermentation takes from seventy-two to ninety-six hours.

Although the product we have been discussing is usually labeled "straight Bourbon," the producer is free to do some artful blending —without a hint on the label to tell of his practices so long as certain limitations are observed. If the mixture consists of Bourbons only, all distilled in the same plant, a blend can be called "straight Bourbon." (The Bourbons in such a blend need not have been distilled at the same time, so long as the brand is labeled with the age of the youngest whiskey used.)

Bonded Bourbon

Because the phrase "bottled in bond" came to have the ring of a guarantee, it was once an important selling point. Bonded whiskey is indeed aged in a warehouse under direct government supervision, but only the proof (100) and age (at least four years) are assured; no quality standard is applied. A fine whiskey when barreled should be a very fine bonded whiskey upon leaving its aging incarceration under Federal auspices, but there is nothing in the regulations to prevent the distiller from starting with poor whiskey.

Once extremely popular, bottled-in-bonds now account for less than 7 per cent of Bourbon consumption, and their sales are still dropping. Their fall from favor, however, is probably due less to consumer recognition of the bonds' limited guarantee of quality than to the growing preference of the consumer for lightness—for the lighter 86-proof (and even 80-proof) straight Bourbons. And indeed, when sipped straight, many bondeds, with their usually fuller body, more positive character, and higher proof, may taste somewhat harsher than many 86-proof Bourbons. This possibility was examined in CU's tests, which brought bonded and nonbonded Bourbons together.

Tennessee whiskey

In terms of mash ingredients, distillation limits, and method and time of aging, "Tennessee" whiskies appear to be just Bourbons distilled in Tennessee. Yet "Bourbon" is found nowhere on their labels. Some experts say they can detect traits that give Tennessees a character of their own—but these distinctions must be rather fine.

Apparently, the Tennessee whiskey people themselves pushed for a ruling making their product different, a non-Bourbon so to speak, evidently for marketing purposes. The Treasury Department powers obliged—more or less. They agreed that it was "not quite a Bourbon" and permitted use of the name "Tennessee whiskey." There isn't any separate standard for the product, however, and subsequent changes in Tennessee whiskey production methods have virtually eliminated whatever differences the distillers were once able to show between their product and "standard" Bourbon. Tennessee whiskies nowadays are Bourbons in all but name.

Tennessee whiskey is filtered through charcoal, which its producers aver gives it a special flavor and mellowness. But this is not necessarily a difference from Bourbon, for it, too, *may* be charcoal-filtered so long as the product conforms to established standards of color, flavor, and character. One whiskey brand tested by CU apparently demonstrates another side of this issue: J. W. Dant Charcoal Perfected Old Style Whiskey is considered a Bourbon by its maker, but the Treasury Department disagrees, and "Bourbon" isn't found on its label.

CU's tests

CU's expert tasters sampled forty-three different whiskies for this section on Bourbons. As usual, the panelists were given the test spirits in coded groups and asked to evaluate the body, aroma, flavor, and overall quality of each sample, as well as to describe taste and aroma characteristics.

The tested products included seven bonded Bourbons (100 proof), four brands of Tennessee whiskey, and thirty-two straight (or blended straight) Bourbons ranging from 80 to 90 proof (mostly 86 or 86.8). Their ages, where listed on the label, ranged from four to ten years. The samples included brands claiming a lineage of more than a century as well as one that was introduced as recently as 1968.

CU's blind tastings of spirits have often turned up unexpected results, and these Bourbon tastings turned up another one: Benchmark, the 1968 newcomer, was judged Very Good in overall quality —and it was the only Bourbon given so high a rating.* Of the other brands, thirty-five were judged Good, and the remaining three were rated Fair. But even though most of the Bourbons were given similar quality ratings, they did not taste alike to the panelists, and the latters' comments (included in the Ratings) may help you find the Bourbon that suits you best.

Most of the Bourbons were judged light-to-intermediate in body. Barclay's was found the lightest; Echo Spring and three of the seven bonded whiskies were considered full-bodied.

The interplay of the closely related characteristics of aroma and taste is complex; as the tasters' comments showed, one won't necessarily tell you anything about the other. Benchmark was the only brand singled out for superior flavor quality. It was variously described as "hearty," "rich, mellow," and "clean" in flavor—but the panelists had nothing to say about its aroma.

Two Bourbons were cited for superior aroma quality—Hiram

---

* Soon after CU's original report on Bourbons was published in the July 1969 issue of CONSUMER REPORTS, Joseph E. Seagram & Sons, manufacturers of Benchmark, published a series of advertisements. These advertisements made certain references to CU's findings as published in CONSUMER REPORTS, in violation of CU's no-commercialization policy. On the basis of these allegedly false and misleading advertisments, Consumers Union thereupon filed suit for injunctive relief and substantial money damages. As of this writing, that litigation is still pending.

Walker's Ten High and J. W. Dant Bonded (the latter evoking particular compliments for aroma richness). Six other brands were judged to have lower-quality aroma, but most of these were not judged correspondingly poor in flavor.

The four Tennessee whiskies were evaluated separately; no significant quality differences emerged—all four were rated Good, as were the majority of tested Bourbons. The two Jack Daniel's versions were judged by the tasters to be of light-to-intermediate body; the two George Dickel whiskies, intermediate-to-full-bodied.

What to buy

Like that of other whiskies, Bourbon quality (as judged by CU's expert tasters) bears little relation to price or age. Bourbon pricing seems to have a strong element of whimsy, in fact. Take alcohol content, a prime cost factor: Six-year-old Seagram's Benchmark, 86 proof, sells at $6.95—same-age Old Hickory Bourbon Bonded, 100 proof, sells at $6. As for the effect, if any, that age has on quality, our tasters found little difference in the broad range of Bourbons rated Good, even between bottles labeled *Eight years old* and those labeled only *Four years old*. If you're not after sipping whiskey quality, you might try one of the brands at the top of the Good group, which is listed in order of ascending price. If you do want sipping whiskey, take a chance on Benchmark, the brand the experts liked best. But don't forget: Your taste may not agree with theirs.

Since the Tennessee whiskies do not, in the judgment of CU's tasters, offer notably higher quality or distinctively different character, it is hard for us to recommend that you try them—especially at their notably higher prices.

Ratings of Bourbon Whiskies

Listed by groups in order of overall quality as judged by CU's expert tasters; within quality groups, listed in order of increasing price. Except as noted, all whiskies are labeled 86 proof; for whiskies of other proof, the cost equivalent of an 86-proof fifth is noted in parentheses. Unless otherwise indicated, prices are recommended retail for a fifth in New York State.

ACCEPTABLE—Very Good

SEAGRAM'S BENCHMARK (Joseph E. Seagram & Sons, Louisville), $6.95. Full flavor.

ACCEPTABLE—Good

BOURBON DE LUXE (The Bourbon De Luxe Distillery Co., Louisville), $4.19 in California. 80 proof ($4.50). Very light aroma. Light flavor.

SUNNY BROOK (Old Sunny Brook Distillery Co., Louisville), $4.29 in California. 80 proof ($4.61).

OLDE BOURBON BY J. W. DANT (The Dant Distillery Co., Aladdin, Pa.), $4.59.

MATTINGLY AND MOORE (Frankfort Distilling Co., Lawrenceburg, Ind.), $4.62. 80 proof ($4.97).

OLD STAGG (Stagg Distilling Co., Frankfort, Ky.), $4.65 in New Jersey. Light flavor.

HIRAM WALKER'S TEN HIGH (Hiram Walker & Sons, Inc., Peoria, Ill.), $4.96. Light flavor.

BARCLAY'S BOURBON (Jas. Barclay & Company, Peoria, Ill.), $4.97. Light body, aroma, and flavor.

ECHO SPRING (Echo Spring Distilling Co., Louisville), $4.99 in California. Full body and aroma.

OLD CROW (The Old Crow Distillery Co., Frankfort, Ky.), $5.06. Light flavor.

ANTIQUE (Frankfort Distilling Co., Louisville), $5.12. Light flavor.

CANADA DRY BOURBON (Canada Dry Distilling Co., Nicholasville, Ky.), $6.40 a quart ($5.12 for an equivalent fifth).

J. W. DANT CHARCOAL PERFECTED OLD STYLE WHISKEY* (The Dant Distillery Co.), $5.19.

KENTUCKY GENTLEMAN (Barton Distilling Co., Bardstown, Ky.), $5.30 in New Jersey. Sweet flavor.

OLD KENTUCKY TAVERN (Glenmore Distilleries Co., Louisville, Ky.), $5.39 in California. Sweet aroma.

BOURBON SUPREME (The American Distilling Co., Inc., Pekin, Ill.), $5.40.

---

* Does not meet standards for Bourbon, according to Treasury Dept.

J. W. DANT BOURBON (The Dant Distillery Co.), $5.49. Full aroma.

HEAVEN HILL (Heaven Hill Distilleries, Inc., Bardstown, Ky.), $5.49. Light aroma and flavor.

OLD HICKORY (Old Hickory Distilling Corp., Philadelphia), $5.55. Light flavor.

YELLOWSTONE (Yellowstone Distillery Co., Louisville), $5.69. 90 proof ($5.44).

EARLY TIMES (Early Times Distillery Co., Louisville), $5.84.

ANCIENT AGE (Ancient Age Distilling Co., Frankfort, Ky.), $5.89.

J. W. DANT BONDED (The Dant Distillery Co.), $5.99. 100 proof ($5.15). Full body and aroma.

OLD CHARTER (Old Charter Distillery Co., Louisville), $5.99 in California. Full aroma and flavor.

OLD HICKORY BOURBON BONDED (Old Hickory Distilling Corp.), $6. 100 proof ($5.16).

WALKER'S DE LUXE BOURBON (Hiram Walker & Sons, Inc.), $6.37. Full aroma. Light flavor.

OLD FORESTER (Brown-Forman Distillers Corp., Louisville), $6.39.

OLD CROW BONDED (The Old Crow Distillery Co.), $6.40 in California. 100 proof ($5.50). Sweet aroma.

OLD TAYLOR (The Old Taylor Distillery Co., Louisville), $6.40. Light aroma and flavor.

BEAM'S CHOICE (James B. Beam Distilling Co., Inc., Clermont-Beam, Ky.), $6.66.

I. W. HARPER (I. W. Harper Distilling Co., Louisville), $6.75. Light flavor.

OLD FITZGERALD (Stitzel-Weller Distillery, Inc., Louisville), $6.91. 86.8 proof ($6.84). Full aroma.

OLD GRAND-DAD (The Old Grand-Dad Distillery Co., Frankfort, Ky.), $7.10. Light flavor.

OLD FORESTER BONDED (Brown-Forman Distillers Corp.), $7.39. 100 proof ($6.36). Full body. Sweet flavor.

I. W. HARPER BONDED (I. W. Harper Distilling Co.), $7.55. 100 proof ($6.49). Full flavor.

OLD TAYLOR BONDED (The Old Taylor Distillery Co.), $7.55. 100 proof ($6.49). Full body.

ACCEPTABLE—Fair

BELLOWS CLUB BOURBON (Bellows & Co., Louisville), $5.45.

JIM BEAM (James B. Beam Distilling Co., Inc.), $5.68.

OLD GRAND-DAD BONDED (The Old Grand-Dad Distillery Co.), $7.55. 100 proof ($6.49).

Ratings of Tennessee Whiskies

ACCEPTABLE—Good

JACK DANIEL'S NO. 7 BRAND TENNESSEE WHISKEY GREEN LABEL (Jack Daniel Distillery, Lynchburg, Tenn.), $6.35 in California. 90 proof ($6.07). Rather light body. Light flavor.

GEORGE DICKEL TENNESSEE SOUR MASH WHISKEY OLD NO. 8 BRAND BLACK LABEL (Geo. A. Dickel & Co., Tullahoma, Tenn.), $6.85. 86.8 proof ($6.77). Rather full body.

JACK DANIEL'S OLD NO. 7 BRAND TENNESSEE SOUR MASH WHIS-KEY BLACK LABEL (Jack Daniel Distillery), $7.80. 90 proof ($7.45). Rather light body.

GEORGE DICKEL TENNESSEE SOUR MASH WHISKEY OLD NO. 12 BRANDY (Geo. A. Dickel & Co.), $7.85. 90 proof ($7.50). Rather full body.

SPIRIT BLENDS AND CANADIANS

American spirit blends and Canadian whiskies are made in different ways. Even so, these two whiskey types have been grouped together in our testing program. Why? Because CU's expert tasters have found it consistently difficult to tell them apart! The experts first encountered this problem when they did their blind tastings of Canadian whiskies and spirit blends for CU's 1958 tests of the products. They ran into it again in more recent tests. Apparently, there's just no getting around it: The two types taste very much alike.

In the light of this finding, it seems rather odd that Americans just about tripled their annual consumption of Canadian whiskies between 1961 and 1971, while sales of spirit blends remained static. And it seems even odder when you consider that prices for the Canadian imports tested are, with one exception, a good bit higher than those for the tested American blends. Have the Canadian whiskies become status symbols for us? Or have we been made to feel that their reputation for mildness puts the Canadian brands in a class by themselves?

Not that they aren't mild, mind you, but CU's taste panel found that, in general, American blended whiskies are just as mild. In fact, it's the lack of any very distinctive flavor or aroma that makes the one type so hard to distinguish from the other. The mildness of the imports is brought about by Canadian distilling methods; the American blends are blended to be mild.

Drinkers of American blends commonly, but inaccurately, call for "rye." Canadian imports, too, are sometimes thought of, erroneously, as rye whiskies. A fair proportion of rye may be used in the making of both product types, but corn, not rye, is almost always the dominant grain. A bartender who filled the ordinary request for "rye" with a straight rye (very few are made) might be heading for trouble, for straight rye has a quite pronounced flavor that is all its own.

Distilling Canadian straight whiskies at about 180 proof (their range is 160–180 proof) is what helps most to assure their mildness. At this relatively high proof, only a limited amount of congeners "comes over" in the distillation process. Then, after they have been aged in barrels, usually for six years or more, the individual whiskies are blended together. All the Canadian whiskies Americans drink are blends, but blends only of various straight whiskies; that is, no neutral spirits are included.

American spirit blends are produced partly from straight whiskies, which are distilled at or below 160 proof and then aged for four years or more. These whiskies usually contain more congeners —and consequently have a rather more decided character—than the whiskies used in the Canadian products. But then the American blender mixes his whiskies with roughly two parts of grain neutral spirits (characterless by law and definition) for each part of straight whiskies. And, with the congeners thus diluted, the pronounced character of the straight whiskies is reduced to a fair degree of mildness. Moreover, if that does not do the trick, American blenders are permitted by law to add up to 2½ per cent by volume of "blending materials" (such as sherry, prune juice, and peach juice) without divulging either their identity or their presence.

The outcome of all this blending, at least among the brands tested, is a line of American spirit blends virtually indistinguishable from the Canadian whiskies, which contain neither neutral spirits nor blending materials.

Test results

At each of several sessions, CU's taste panelists were given both spirit blends and Canadians, identified only by code numbers. The tasters were asked to judge whether each sample was an American blend, a Canadian, or some other type of spirit (actually, no other type was used). Results: The tasters called some blends Canadians, noted some Canadians as blends, and suggested that some samples of both types might be very mild Scotch or Bourbon.

The panelists also had great difficulty in differentiating among the various brands. The tasters were asked to evaluate each sample in terms of bouquet, flavor, body, and overall quality. The net result was, in a word, sameness. All of the tested brands were judged to be roughly equal in overall quality.

This is not to say that all the brands tasted exactly alike to CU's experts; they didn't. But in only eight of the twenty-seven brands tested could most panel members consistently detect particular and unique characteristics. And, in the taster's view, even these signs of individuality were not distinct enough to render any whiskey significantly different from the others or to influence the rating scores significantly. As a result, it was decided that no quality ratings could be given.

CU's testers sampled the brands diluted 50/50 with distilled water, and at room temperature. Add more water, soda, or some other mixer to these brands (as in making a highball), and the minute differences found by CU's panelists become, of course, still less noticeable. Even the addition of ice alone makes them harder to distinguish, for the chill dulls the taste buds.

[2]ᵗ

What to buy

The advice of CU is that you buy by price when you go shopping for one of these mild whiskies—unless you're dead set on impressing friends. You can pay up to $9.80 for one of the Canadian brands tested, but why should you when you can get one of the taste-alike American brands for no more than $5.55 and for as little as $4.29? Since the proofs ranged widely from 80 to 90, we have included the actual amount of alcohol and the cost per ounce of alcohol in the listing of each brand.

Listings of Canadian and American Blend Whiskies

These spirits were found to be uniformly light in aroma, flavor, and body with minor differences not significant enough for quality ratings. Within types, listed in order of increasing price per fifth and alphabetically at each price level. All the American blends are 86 proof unless otherwise indicated. Prices are recommended retail prices in New York State.

CANADIAN WHISKIES

BARTON'S CANADIAN MIST (Barton Distillers Import Co., N.Y.C.), $5.29. Bottled in U.S. 80 proof. 10.2 oz. of alcohol (52¢ per oz.).

CANADIAN LORD CALVERT (Calvert Distilling Co., Relay, Md.), $5.91. Bottled in U.S. 80 proof. 10.2 oz. of alcohol (58¢ per oz.).

MacNAUGHTON (Schenley Imports Co., N.Y.C.), $6.19. Bottled in U.S. 86.8 proof. 11.1 oz. of alcohol (56¢ per oz.).

OLD MR. BOSTON CANADIAN RIVER (Mr. Boston Distiller, Inc., Boston), $6.39. Bottled in U.S. 86.8 proof. 11.1 oz. of alcohol (58¢ per oz.).

O.F.C. BY SCHENLEY (Canadian Schenley Distilling Co., N.Y.C.), $7.40. Bottled in Canada. 86.8 proof. 11.1 oz. of alcohol (67¢ per oz.).

SEAGRAM'S V.O. (Seagram Distillers Co., N.Y.C.), $7.40. Bottled in Canada. 86.8 proof. 11.1 oz. of alcohol (67¢ per oz.).

CANADIAN CLUB (Hiram Walker Importers Inc., Detroit), $7.41. Bottled in Canada. 86.8 proof. 11.1 oz. of alcohol (67¢ per oz.).

SEAGRAM'S CROWN ROYAL (Seagram Distillers Co.), $9.80. Bottled in Canada. 80 proof. 10.2 oz. of alcohol (96¢ per oz.).

AMERICAN BLENDS

OLD THOMPSON (Glenmore Distilleries Co., Owensboro, Ky.), $4.29. 11.0 oz. of alcohol (39¢ per oz.).

MR. BOSTON'S PINCH (Mr. Boston Distiller, Inc.), $4.35. 80 proof. 10.2 oz. of alcohol (42¢ per oz.).

G & W SEVEN STAR (Hiram Walker & Sons, Inc., Peoria, Ill.), $4.50. 80 proof. 10.2 oz. of alcohol (44¢ per oz.).

CARSTAIRS WHITE SEAL (Carstairs Distilling Co., Baltimore), $4.60. 80 proof. 10.2 oz. of alcohol (45¢ per oz.).

BARTON'S RESERVE (Barton Distilling Co., Bardstown, Ky.), $4.65. 90 proof. 11.5 oz. of alcohol (40¢ per oz.).

GUCKENHEIMER RESERVE (American Distilling Co., Inc., Pekin, Ill.), $4.69. 84 proof. 10.8 oz. of alcohol (44¢ per oz.).

WILSON "THAT'S ALL" (Wilson Distilling Co., Louisville), $4.76. 80 proof. 10.2 oz. of alcohol (46¢ per oz.).

BELLOWS RESERVE (Bellows & Co., Cincinnati), $4.90. 11.0 oz. of alcohol (45¢ per oz.).

PARK & TILFORD RESERVE (Park & Tilford Distillers Co., Aladdin, Pa.), $4.95. 80 proof. 10.2 oz. of alcohol (48¢ per oz.).

CORBY'S RESERVE (Jas. Barclay & Co., Peoria, Ill.), $4.96. 11.0 oz. of alcohol (45¢ per oz.).

IMPERIAL (Hiram Walker & Sons, Inc.), $4.96. 11.0 oz. of alcohol (45¢ per oz.).

PHILADELPHIA (Continental Distilling Co., Philadelphia), $4.98. 11.0 oz. of alcohol (45¢ per oz.).

KESSLER (Julius Kessler Co., Lawrenceburg, Ind.), $5. 11.0 oz. of alcohol (45¢ per oz.).

FLEISCHMANN'S PREFERRED (Fleischmann Distilling Corp., Peekskill, N.Y.), $5.08. 90 proof. 11.5 oz. of alcohol (44¢ per oz.).

MELROSE RARE DIAMOND "12" (Melrose & Co., Aladdin, Pa.), $5.40. 11.0 oz. of alcohol (49¢ per oz.).

CALVERT EXTRA (Calvert Distilling Co., Baltimore), $5.55. 11.0 oz. of alcohol (50¢ per oz.).

FOUR ROSES (Four Roses Distilling Co., Louisville), $5.55. 11.0 oz. of alcohol (50¢ per oz.).

SCHENLEY RESERVE (Schenley Distillers Inc., Schenley, Pa.), $5.55. 11.0 oz. of alcohol (50¢ per oz.).

SEAGRAM'S 7 CROWN (Joseph E. Seagram & Sons, Lawrenceburg, Ind.), $5.55. 11.0 oz. of alcohol (50¢ per oz.).

~~~~~~

Chapter 11

VODKA, GIN, AND OTHER WHITE SPIRITS

First, a few before-and-after statistics. Less than twenty years ago, in 1954, whiskey—Scotch, Bourbon, the spirit blends, and the others—accounted for 82 per cent of all liquor sales made in this country. By contrast, sales of vodka were so meager that, until 1950, the Treasury Department didn't bother to keep separate records on vodka bottling. But then came the change—to "mildness." By 1971 whiskey sales had dropped to 62 per cent of the total, whereas vodka sales had risen to 14 per cent and those of gin to around 10 per cent. Meanwhile, total liquor sales had themselves doubled.

In turning to vodka and gin the public was simply carrying its quest for mildness to a logical conclusion. Both spirits blend quite well with just about any mixer—there is little danger that either of them will overpower the mixer. Vodka in particular is almost completely devoid of flavor.

CU tested a representative selection of vodkas and gins. For the other white spirits (tequila, akvavit) no testing was done, but brands suggested by CU's consultants have been listed.

VODKA

The popular conception of vodka as the national drink of Russia is certainly accurate, although both Russia and Poland claim credit for having invented it. Less accurate is the notion that vodka, or even Russian vodka, is made from potatoes (though it can be). Today it is usually made from grain, and some vodka was produced from grain even in Imperial Russia.

In 1968–69 the Treasury Department revised its standards for vodka and gin. According to its new regulations, the distiller may make vodka in any way he chooses so long as the end product is "neutral spirits so distilled, or so treated after distillation with charcoal or other materials, as to be without distinctive character, aroma, taste, or color, and bottled at not less than 80 proof." As noted earlier, "neutral spirits" are, by definition, distilled from any material whatever at or above 190 proof, and the regulations further require merely that the material's type or category be disclosed on the label as grain, fruit, cane products, etc.

Since neutral spirits have so little character, the mash ingredients that the distillers select for them are understandably the handiest and cheapest (in terms of sugar yield) available. Corn and sorghum quite often fill the bill in this country.

CU's tests

Our expert tasters sampled six national and four private-label brands to put to the test CU's hypothesis that given its prescribed lack of "distinctive character," vodka was one spirit that could definitely be bought by price alone. They also tested an imported Russian vodka, at both its original 100 proof and, after it had been cut with distilled water, at 80 proof. Finally, some of the coded samples didn't come out of a vodka bottle at all: They consisted of a laboratory grade of pure ethyl alcohol cut to drinkable proof with distilled water.

The panelists were asked to rate each sample for smoothness and overall quality, but they were not asked to evaluate taste, since vodka is essentially tasteless. Despite breathless claims of producers, however, it is not really odorless, so the tasters were also asked to rate each sample for aroma off-notes (any bouquet other than the distinctive odor of pure alcohol).

The experts' favorite vodka? It turned out to be the diluted laboratory-grade alcohol. The panelists found it smoothest to the palate, lowest in aroma off-note presence, and highest in overall quality.

None of the ten domestic vodkas was found to differ substantially from the others, although Smirnoff was judged to be very slightly smoother than the rest and Wolfschmidt to have somewhat fainter aroma off-notes. The differences were too slight to affect the ratings, however, and neither brand matched the laboratory-grade alcohol.

The panelists found rather more character in the imported Stolichnaya at 100 proof—and they didn't like it. Some tasters thought this vodka harsh, others found it left an unpleasant aftertaste—reactions that perhaps had their roots in the extra bit of higher proof. Diluted to 80 proof, Stolichnaya aroused no adverse comment (it's now sold both at 100 and 80 proof).

What to buy

When you buy vodka, you're buying alcohol. Since laboratory-grade ethyl alcohol isn't generally available for beverage use, you might as well settle for the least expensive brand of vodka you can find. Consider first the private-label brands available in many liquor stores (although not necessarily in the "control" states, which decide which brands will be sold). The private-label brands will almost always offer a saving.

If you think that you might like a small degree of flavor and aroma (and feel like paying double or so for the pleasure), you might try Stolichnaya or some other Slavic import. But if you're not going to down it neat, keep in mind that our experts were hard put to tell Stolichnaya apart from any of the domestic brands after water had been added to it to lower the proof. (Some Slavic vodkas are specially flavored; Zubrovka, for example, a Polish product, is flavored with buffalo grass, a blade of which is often left in the bottle.) Remember to look for the proof on imported vodkas—many are sold only at 100 proof.

Proof and price

Finding the best buy in a given brand of vodka can be a little tricky, CU discovered. Many vodkas come in both fifths and quarts, and at both 80 and 100 proof, so you can't simply compare price tags alone. The price per ounce of *alcohol* is the key factor, although our price-check might lead one to wonder whether the distributors realize it is. For a given brand, you might expect to save a little money by buying a quart rather than a fifth at the same proof, but some quarts actually priced out at more per ounce than the fifth did. Likewise, you might at least expect the alcohol price to remain the same if you buy at 100 rather than 80 proof, but one brand ran more per ounce of alcohol at the higher proof.

Luckily we can offer you a shortcut to make these comparisons without fancy mathematics.* If a fifth and a quart are the same proof, add one-fourth more to the price of the fifth (for example, add $1 if the fifth costs $4). If the quart price is less than your total ($5, in our example), you'll save money buying it. This same calculation works in comparing the same size bottles, one at 80 proof and one at 100 proof. Add one-fourth to the price of the 80 proof—you'll save if the 100 proof costs less than the new total. (Note: An 80-proof quart and a 100-proof fifth contain the same amount of alcohol and should therefore be expected to cost just about the same.)

If you do buy on this cost-per-ounce-of-alcohol basis, you'll only preserve your savings if you use less 100-proof vodka in a drink than you would of 80-proof—specifically, about four-fifths as much. (It might help your equilibrium, too.) If you find this too minor a detail to bother with, you're better off finding the best buy you can at 80 proof and sticking with the jigger size that makes your drinks the strength you like.

---

* *On the other hand, if you're a whiz at math, you can work from these facts: A fifth of 80-proof vodka contains 10.24 ounces of alcohol; a quart, 12.8 ounces. A fifth of 100-proof vodka contains 12.8 ounces of alcohol; a quart, 16 ounces.*

Listing of Vodkas

Listed in order of increasing price per fifth, since no significant quality differences were found. All domestic vodkas listed are 80 proof; many brands are also available at 100 proof. Prices for national brands are recommended retail for New York State; for private-label brands, those paid by CU's shoppers.

MACY'S 734 (Private-label brand for R. H. Macy & Co., N.Y.C.), $3.81 a quart ($3.05 for equivalent fifth).

RED CROWN (Private-label brand for the Great Atlantic & Pacific Tea Co., Inc., N.Y.C.), $3.25.

GREELEY SQUARE (Private-label brand purchased at Gimbel Bros., Inc., N.Y.C.), $3.89.

BACK BAY (Private-label brand for Sherry-Lehmann, Inc., N.Y.C.), $3.98.

MAJORSKA (Clyde-Stafford, Nutley, N.J.), $3.99.

GORDON'S (Distillers Co., Ltd., Linden, N.J.), $4.29.

WOLFSCHMIDT (Wolfschmidt, Dundalk, Md.), $4.35.

FLEISCHMANN'S (Fleischmann Distilling Corp., Peekskill, N.Y.), $4.41.

SAMOVAR (Boaka Kompaniya, Schenley, Pa.), $5.15.

SMIRNOFF (Heublein, Inc., Hartford, Conn.) $5.40.

STOLICHNAYA RUSSIAN VODKA (Kraus Bros. & Co., Philadelphia), $7.99. 100 proof.

GIN

Gin got its start as a medicine, invented by a seventeenth-century Dutch physician, Franciscus de la Boe, also known as Dr. Sylvius. It was the doctor's intention to develop an inexpensive medicine incorporating the oil of the juniper berry, which he knew had diuretic properties. To achieve his objective, he added the berries to pure alcohol and redistilled the latter. How effective a diuretic his concoction was, we cannot say, but "Genever"—as he called it after the berry's French name, genièvre—quickly came to public notice in Holland, where it was eventually used to treat many more ailments than the good doctor could have imagined.

Toward the end of the century, Genever, already familiar to British soldiery abroad, found its way to England, where its name was shortened to gin. It took that country, too, by storm. There, though, its success was hastened by England's king, William of Orange, who was determined to see the Dutch product supplant French brandy in the hearts of his new countrymen.

Gin underwent some changes, however, in its translation from the Dutch original, which was and is a full-bodied and full-flavored spirit with a malty taste and aroma. In Britain, becoming ever lighter in body and flavor, it finally evolved into what is now called "London dry" or just plain "dry" gin. It is made in much the same way in both the British Isles and the United States.

There are thus two basic types of gin* produced today: dry gin and Dutch gin. We know the latter as Hollands gin, but in the Netherlands it is still usually called Genever or sometimes Schiedam, after a Dutch town prominent in gin-making. It is flavored almost exclusively with juniper berries and distilled at a very low proof, under 110. Those who like it take it neat; its pronounced taste would probably drown out that of a mixer. Very little Hollands gin is seen in the United States, and CU did not test any. This report deals only with dry gin, the spirit of the dry martini.

Dry gin

Basically, dry gin is subtly flavored vodka. American producers start with neutral spirits distilled at 190 proof or above; the British use alcohol distilled at around 180–188. It is the slightly greater amount of congeners that comes over into the British distillate that, in large part, accounts for any differences discernible between British and domestic gins. The somewhat dissimilar mineral contents of American and British water are also reputed to affect the alcohol, but this is a matter of conjecture.

Whether British or American, the alcohol is diluted with distilled water and then redistilled with an infusion of botanical

---

* *Sloe gin is not a gin at all, but a cordial flavored with sloe berries (see Chapter 14). Old Tom gin, once popular but now rarely made, is a sweetened gin prepared by adding sugar to conventional dry gin.*

flavoring agents. (Redistillation is not, however, required by the new Federal standards for gin. Flavors and essences may now simply be mixed with the alcohol—a shortcut process that previously required the unappetizing designation "compound gin." Gins that *are* still produced by redistillation may be labeled "distilled.") Juniper is always the dominant flavor, but the other botanicals are chosen from a wide array of herbs and spices: citrus peels, fennel, anise or licorice, cardamom, caraway, coriander, and so on. The botanicals are either put in directly with the spirits being redistilled or suspended at the top of the still, where the rising alcohol vapors can pick up their volatile essential oils.

The producer's "secret formula," his choice of which botanicals to use and in what proportions, may well be the most important factor influencing his product's aroma, taste, and quality. Judicially selected botanicals can even reinforce the *impression* the drinker receives of a given gin's dryness. But they cannot make that gin actually drier than other gins or drier than it was to start with, for all gins are rendered equally dry (that is, lacking in sweetness) by the way they are made, botanicals or no. The words *London* or *London Dry* on an American gin label mean only that the brand is supposed to be similar in character to gins produced in London or thereabouts. Just how similar American and British gins are was one of the questions our blind tastings set out to answer.

Gins do not have to be aged, and no specific age claims may legally be made for them. A few brands are aged but were not included in this project. In past tests, CU judged them not to differ significantly from other brands except in the golden color that aging had given them.

CU's tests

The twenty-three brands of dry gin tested included eleven domestic gins with national distribution, four private-label domestic gins found in the New York metropolitan area, and eight imported gins.

As in other CU tests of spirits, the panel of expert tasters was given "blind" samples, identified only by code numbers. To assure consistency of comparisons, the various gins were presented in different combinations at each tasting session. Duplicate, but differently coded, samples of each brand were included. The panelists based their overall quality ratings on evaluations of smoothness and the strength, quality, and character of aroma and flavor. In the course of their blind tasting, they were obliged to guess whether each sample was a domestic or an imported gin.

Despite abundant advertising of the superiorities of imported gins, our experts were baffled when it came to pinning down the origin of a particular sample. Imported Beefeater, for example, was identified as an import less than 15 per cent of the time. Coates Plymouth was recognized in 50 per cent of its samples for the import it is, but this finding may be related to the fact that Plymouth gin is made by a process said to be intermediate between dry gin and Dutch gin processes. (The experts, though, had no particular comments on Plymouth.) On the other hand, the domestic Seagram's Extra Dry—which the panelists liked—was usually identified, incorrectly, as an imported brand. The origin of only one brand—a domestic private-label—was consistently identified correctly. These results tend to support the notion that adroit botanical choices are more important in giving a brand of gin whatever individuality it may have than differences in British and American distillation methods.

The tasters had difficulty not only in guessing gin origins but also in making any marked distinctions among the brands in flavor and aroma. Only a few brands received particular comment: Seagram's Extra Dry was felt to hold a slight edge in overall quality over the other gins. Although its aroma and flavor strengths were judged somewhat lower than average, the panelists rated it a trifle higher than the others in aroma and flavor qualities and smoothness. Nicholson's Lamplighter and Booth's House of Lords (both imported) were found somewhat smoother than the remaining brands—but at a sacrifice in flavor strength. Gordon's and Melrose (both domestic) were judged less smooth than most, possibly because they also impressed the panel as having somewhat stronger-than-average flavors.

What to buy

The experts found it fairly hard to detect differences in quality between imported and domestic gins, but no one should have any trouble spotting the differences between them in price. The lowest-priced import cost over 60 cents more than the *most expensive* nationally distributed domestic brand, even allowing for the import's somewhat higher proof. At the other end of the price picture, the private-label brands tested offered savings of 25 cents to $1 over the *least expensive* national brand tested.

Since the price differences are so much more conspicuous than the quality differences were found to be—and since the latter would have been even more elusive had the experts tested the gins in mixed drinks instead of straight—CU recommends that you consider buying the lowest-priced gin you can find. To compare costs of fifths and quarts at the same proof, you can apply one of the guidelines given for vodka buying (see page 144): The price of the quart should be *less* than 25 per cent above that for the corresponding fifth.

If you drink your gin straight, or with relatively bland mixers, it's possible that you could recognize a familiar gin on the first drink. (But don't bet on it, at least not until you have attempted the triangle test outlined on page 11.) With the second drink, however—what with the dulling effect of alcohol and cold on the taste buds and the masking effect of vermouth or some other mixer on the flavor of gin—chances are good that any distinctiveness the gin may have had would vanish.

Listing of Gins

Listed in order of increasing price per fifth and alphabetically at each price level, since no significant quality differences were found.

Except as noted, all are 90 proof. For gins of other proof, the cost equivalent of a 90-proof fifth is noted in parentheses. Prices for national brands are recommended retail for New York State, except as noted; for private-label brands, those paid by CU's shoppers. Country of origin is shown for imported brands.

RED CROWN (Private-label brand for the Great Atlantic & Pacific Tea Co., Inc., N.Y.C.), $3.25.

MACY'S RED STAR DISTILLED DRY (Private-label brand for R. H. Macy & Co., N.Y.C.), $4.75 a quart ($3.80 for an equivalent fifth).

BACK BAY DISTILLED DRY (Private-label brand for Sherry-Lehmann, Inc., N.Y.C.), $3.98.

PARKLEIGH DELUXE DISTILLED LONDON DRY (Private-label brand for Gimbel Bros., Inc., N.Y.C.), $3.99.

DIXIE BELLE DISTILLED (Continental Distilling Co., Philadelphia), $4.25 in New Jersey.

MELROSE DISTILLED LONDON DRY (Melrose & Co., Aladdin, Pa.), $4.40 in New Jersey.

WALKER'S CRYSTAL DRY (Hiram Walker & Sons, Inc., Peoria, Ill.), $4.66.

CANADA DRY DISTILLED LONDON DRY (Canada Dry Distilling Co., Nicholasville, Ky.), $4.69.

SCHENLEY EXTRA DRY (Schenley Distillers, Inc., Schenley, Pa.), $4.79.

FLEISCHMANN'S DISTILLED DRY (Fleischmann Distilling Corp., Peekskill, N.Y.), $4.80.

CALVERT DISTILLED LONDON DRY (Calvert Distilling Co., Baltimore), $4.85.

GILBEY'S DISTILLED LONDON DRY (W. & A. Gilbey, Ltd., Cincinnati), $4.95.

GORDON'S DISTILLED LONDON DRY (Renfield Importers, Ltd., N.Y.C.), $4.95.

SEAGRAM'S EXTRA DRY (Jos. E. Seagram & Sons, Lawrenceburg, Ind.), $4.95.

BOOTH'S HIGH & DRY DISTILLED LONDON DRY (Booth Distilleries, Linden, N.J.), $5.11.

JOHN POWER'S DISTILLED DRY (Canada Dry Corp., N.Y.C.), $5.99 in New Jersey. 94 proof ($5.73). Irish.

OLD GENTRY DISTILLED LONDON DRY (Van Munching Importers, Inc., N.Y.C.), $6.08. 94.8 proof ($5.77). Scottish.

J & B DISTILLED LONDON DRY (Paddington Corp., N.Y.C.), $6.25 in California. 91.4 proof ($6.15). English.

NICHOLSON'S LAMPLIGHTER ENGLISH DRY (McKesson & Robbins, Inc., N.Y.C.), $6.35. 94 proof ($6.08). English.
BOOTH'S HOUSE OF LORDS DISTILLED DRY (W. A. Taylor & Co., N.Y.C.), $6.41. 86 proof ($6.71). English.
COATES PLYMOUTH DISTILLED DRY (Schenley Imports Co., N.Y.C.), $6.60. 94.4 proof ($6.29). English.
BEEFEATER LONDON DISTILLED DRY (Kobrand Corp., N.Y.C.), $6.70. 94 proof ($6.41). English.
TANQUERAY SPECIAL DRY DISTILLED ENGLISH (James M. McCunn & Co., Inc., N.Y.C.), $6.75. 94.6 proof ($6.42). English.

TEQUILA

Americans have lately been getting acquainted with Mexico's national drink in growing numbers, and many seem to like it. Tequila is made from a species of agave, a cactuslike plant related to the century plant. The white spirit from south of the border has a partially deserved fiery reputation, which may be related to the fact that Mexicans take it straight—in a manner of speaking. Tequila is, in Mexican tradition, the center of a ceremony in which the drink is gulped down after the tongue has been primed with lime (or lemon) juice and salt.

Most Americans prefer to do their mixing in the glass, and the mixture they like best is the unfiery but hardly innocuous margarita: tequila, triple sec, and lime or lemon juice, shaken with ice and strained into a salt-rimmed cocktail glass (recipe, page 201). Because tequila is so closely tied to a single cocktail, some liquor-industry observers consider tequila as just a splash in the pan. It was nevertheless a good-sized splash in 1971: Well over a million gallons of tequila were imported. Since 1969 we have had a formal U.S. definition of tequila.*

The name is derived from the town of Tequila, northwest of

* *The standard of identity defines tequila as "an alcoholic distillate from fermented mash derived principally from the Agave tequilana Weber (blue variety), with or without additional fermentable substances, distilled in such manner that the distillate possesses the taste, aroma, and characteristics generally attributed to tequila and bottled at not less than 80 proof, and also includes mixtures solely of such distillates."*

Guadalajara in the Mexican state of Jalisco; the term is limited by the Mexican government to products distilled in or near that town. (Roughly the same spirit is produced elsewhere in Mexico, but called mescal, after a local name for the plant from which it is derived. Mainly for home consumption, mescal tends to be rather less smooth than tequila; it is not for the faint-hearted.)

Agave tequilana takes about twelve years to mature. The base or heart of the plant looks rather like an oversized pineapple and is laden with a sugary juice called aguamiel—"honey water." Cut from the plant and split open at the distillery, the agave "pineapples" are oven-heated for half a day or so. Part of the aguamiel oozes out during heating; then the hearts are shredded and pressed to extract the remaining sap. The aguamiel is then fermented in large vats for 2½ to 3 days, using spent mash or new yeast to initiate fermentation. The fermented product is pot-distilled twice, brought over at a low proof—usually 104. Tequila may be bottled immediately, or it may be aged in oak vats for anywhere from six months to four years. A slight amber in some aged tequilas may come from such barreling (though it could, of course, just be caramel.) Most of the brands seen in the United States have been bottled at 80 proof, though a few are somewhat higher.

Listing of Tequilas

Tequilas were not tested. The best-known national brands are listed here in order of increasing price per fifth. Prices are recommended retail for New York State.

GAVILAN WHITE (Foreign Vintages, Inc., N.Y.C.), $6.20. 90 proof.

PEPE LOPEZ (Jos. Garneau Co., N.Y.C.), $6.45. 80 proof.

SAUZA SILVER (National Distillers Products Co., N.Y.C.), $6.49. 80 proof.

EL TORO (American Distilling Co., N.Y.C.), $6.69. 80 proof.

MARIACHI (Distillers Corp.-Seagrams Ltd., Montreal), $6.71. 80 proof.

JOSE CUERVO WHITE (Heublein, Inc., Hartford, Conn.), $6.75. 86 proof.

AKVAVIT

Akvavit is to the Scandinavians pretty much what vodka is to the Russians. Usually quaffed ice cold, in a single gulp, akvavit is generally served with smörgasbord or other food and is sometimes followed by a chaser of beer. Interest in this spirit is limited, though increasing, in the United States, where some hosts and hostesses serve it with appetizers as a party-opener.

The name akvavit (also spelled "aquavit") is derived from the Latin *aqua vitae* ("water of life"). In thirteenth-century Italy, the phrase was applied to the earliest spirits distilled from wine. Grapes don't grow in chilly Scandinavia; so spirits were uncommon there until soldiers returned with the secrets of distilling from grain. Poor grain harvests meant no akvavit, however, until the distillers hit on the potato.

Akvavit is distilled in all four Scandinavian countries, mostly from potatoes but also (especially for exports) from grain. The resulting neutral spirit is diluted and redistilled with flavoring agents, much as gin is flavored in redistillation. Instead of juniper berries, the dominant flavoring in akvavit is caraway seed. Cardamom, citrus peels, aniseed, and other flavorings are also employed, sparingly. It is usually bottled at about 90 proof.

Generally speaking, akvavit is similar in taste to the cordial known as kümmel (see Chapter 14), but without the liqueur's added sugar. Akvavit is not really a fixed product type in Scandinavia; witness the twenty or so brands turned out in Sweden. Some are sweetened, some are unsweetened, some are aged, and some are unaged, and some are even fruit-flavored. In general, the few imported and distributed here are alike—dry, strong, and with a pronounced caraway flavor.

Listing of Akvavits

Akvavits were not tested. Three widely distributed brands are listed below, in order of increasing price. Prices are recommended retail for New York State.

BOMMERLUNDER (German Distillers, Ltd., N.Y.C.), $6.97 (fifth). 80 proof.

AALBORG TAFFEL (Munson G. Shaw Co., N.Y.C.), $6.99 (24 oz.). 90 proof.

O. P. ANDERSON'S (Standard Wine & Liquor Co., Inc., N.Y.C.), $7.39 (fifth). 86 proof.

Chapter 12

RUM

T he history of rum starts with Columbus, who brought sugar cane to the West Indies. The early Spanish settlers there lost little time in experimenting with a sugar cane distillate that became known as rum.

Easy to make from the readily accessible West Indian molasses, and consequently low in cost, rum quickly won acceptance with many Americans in colonial times, particularly in New England where large quantities of it were distilled. A waggish Dartmouth College song toasts its founder, Eleazar Wheelock, whose ". . . whole curriculum, was 500 gallons of New England rum." It has never been as popular since.

Perhaps rum has suffered from its association with drunken sailors or from the nineteenth-century use of its name to mean, in a pejorative sense, any spirit, as in "Demon rum." The very word "rum" is, according to Webster's, "perhaps" a short form of the obsolete term "rumbullion," which meant a fracas or uproar. Some authorities, however, doubt that this was the word's origin; CU's consultants prefer to believe that the word derives, more sedately, from the last syllable of the Latin word for sugar, *saccharum*.

Rum more than tripled in U.S. sales in the last fifteen years, but it still occupies only a tiny corner (3.4 per cent) of the spirits market, and even that chiefly in its light-bodied form (as a base for daiquiris and other mixed drinks). The light-bodied rums are produced mostly in Puerto Rico and the U.S. Virgin Islands. The full-bodied rums are traditionally associated with Jamaica, Demerara, Barbados, and other Caribbean points (not including Haiti and Martinique, whose rums are generally intermediate in body). But you *can,* as CU discovered, get a full-bodied Puerto Rican rum, so that buying simply by country of origin isn't an absolute guarantee that you'll end up with the type you want. Price may be a safer guideline: The least expensive full-bodied rum almost invariably costs more than the most expensive light-bodied rum (unless the latter is "specially flavored").

As with other types of spirits, the main difference between one rum and another is determined by the amounts and kinds of congeners in the liquor—the substances that remain with the alcohol in the distillation process and give it flavor, aroma, body, and (to a very limited extent) color. Light-bodied rums are generally distilled at a higher proof than full-bodied rums and hence are lower in congeners. CU's taste-tests were limited to the light-bodied group because the dark rums, as the full-bodied brands are often called, have so few purchasers here. This chapter does include, however, a brief discussion of both the full-bodied and the intermediate-bodied types.

LIGHT-BODIED RUMS

Since the break in relations between the United States and Cuba, nearly all the light-bodied rums we drink—and they make up over 95 per cent of the total amount of rum consumed here—come from Puerto Rico and the Virgin Islands. These rums are reasonably dry, and they are almost invariably bottled at 80 proof.

Production begins with the molasses left over after sugar has been made from sugar cane. This molasses residue, which retains as much as 50 per cent of fermentable sugar, is pumped into large fermentation vats. Water, cultured yeast, and spent "beer" from a previous fermentation are added to get the ferment going. The process lasts two to four days. Then the mash is filtered and distilled in a column still at a fairly high proof—usually between 180 and 190, though it can be as low as 160. Distillation at the higher proofs pretty well assure a light-bodied product with a limited amount of flavor.

Virgin Islands rums generally are not aged at all. Puerto Rican rums are usually aged at least four years, but they don't have to be. (Commonwealth law prescribes a one-year minimum for light rums, three years for dark rums.) Most rums are blends of different lots, whether aged or not.

The color of the rum hasn't much to do with aging (or the lack of it), for the uncharred wooden barrels employed impart little color to the spirits. A rum's complexion depends, rather, on the amount of caramel coloring added, and that amount is supposed to reflect whether the rum is more on the light-bodied or on the full-bodied side. The color coding extends to descriptions on the labels as well: Light-colored rums usually carry the phrase *White* (or *Silver*) *Label;* darker rums, the phrase *Amber* (or *Gold*) *Label.* Further, the labels are usually colored to suit the terminology.

CU's tests of light-bodied rums

Thirteen widely sold brands of light-bodied rums—from both Puerto Rico and the Virgin Islands—were evaluated in blind tastings by CU's panel of experts (this represents only a sampling of the brands and versions available). The project covered the typical price range for these products in New York State, and comprised both light-*colored* and dark-*colored* rums (though all were light-*bodied*). To shed some light on the relationship between color differences and taste differences, a few color pairs (light and dark versions of the same brand) were included among the selections.

As a check on the panelists' taste buds, there were also slipped into the samples—but not into the Ratings—two light-bodied rums* that were "specially flavored" and a Puerto Rican rum**

---

* *Bacardi Anejo, found "artificial" but very smooth, and Don Q Eldorado, described as having a slightly "musty" (but pleasant) aroma and flavor. Both at 80 proof, about $6.50 a fifth.*
** *Ron del Barrilito, judged to have a far stronger aroma than the average light-bodied rum, with an "unusual" flavor. To be sipped straight or on-the-rocks. At 86 proof, about $8 a fifth.*

reputed to be very full-bodied (unlike most rums from that island). The tasters had no trouble spotting the three intruders.

Comparisons of color pairs indicated that the blenders weren't always successful in matching color with taste. Thus, pairs of Virgin Islands rums, according to CU's consultants, do not differ by much more than their coloring, the darker member of each pair usually being no more full-bodied than the light.

Among the thirteen light-bodied rums, none was considered outstandingly good or bad in any particular characteristic, but differences in overall quality (which in even the lowest-rated brand was deemed satisfactory) were found to be sufficient to allow ranking of the rums.

Highest marks went to dark-colored Bacardi Amber Label, a Puerto Rican product, but its brand-mate, light-colored Bacardi Silver Label, was thought only middling in overall quality. This brand-pair appears also to be a case of mismatched color and taste: The experts judged the top-rated Amber not as strong in flavor as the Silver, though slightly stronger in aroma.

Significant quality differences were also found in another pair of brand-mates, but with the taste and color more appropriately matched. Don Q White Label, although still quite acceptable, wound up last in overall quality, whereas Don Q Gold Label was a runner-up for the number-one spot. The Gold was judged to have more and higher-quality aroma than its lighter sibling and was also found much smoother.

In a third brand-pair, Boca Chica, the panelists again preferred the darker version. They found the Gold Label high in aroma quality—not so the light White Label. The Gold Label was judged average in smoothness, lower than average in flavor strength; the White Label, judged very low in flavor strength, was the smoothest rum tested (possibly because of its weak flavor).

Because Puerto Rican rums are aged, they are supposed to be better than the typically unaged rums from the Virgin Islands. On the whole, this supposition was supported by the experts' blind tastings. But not all Puerto Rican rums tasted were found higher in overall quality than all three tested Virgin Islands products, and one of the latter (Brugal White) was ranked sixth among the thirteen entries—or better than five Puerto Rican rums tested.

What to buy

Each of the two top-scorers costs around a dollar more per fifth than does the lowest-priced brand in the project, the Old St. Croix White. But before you decide that for you the difference in quality is worth the difference in price, remember that the panelists judged even the bottom-ranked entry not greatly lower in overall quality than the leaders. Remember, too, that your taste may not agree with the panelists'; and try the triangle test on page 11—you may find you're unable to detect *any* differences. Finally, if you're like most other light-rum drinkers, you'll be using your rum principally, if not altogether, in mixed drinks—in which case the differences the experts noted (in *straight* samples) will be less conspicuous, even to the point of nonexistence.

Speaking of mixed drinks, another decision you'll have to make is whether you want to buy light-bodied rum, for daiquiris, etc., or full-bodied, for planter's punch and hot buttered rum. Or both. (The better-quality full-bodied rums are also, in many quarters, sipped neat.) And, by the way, if you make your daiquiris with one of the *Amber-* or *Gold-Label* rums, they may be darker in color than the daiquiris you're likely to get from your neighborhood bartender—he's apt to use a *White-* or *Silver-Label* rum in his, albeit for no very worthwhile reason that CU can figure out.

Ratings of Light-Bodied Rums

Listed in order of estimated overall quality, as judged by CU's expert tasters. Closely ranked brands did not differ significantly. All rums listed are 80 proof. Prices are recommended retail for New York State. Origins of rums are abbreviated—Puerto Rico (P.R.) and Virgin Islands (V.I.).

RON BACARDI AMBER (Bacardi Corp., San Juan, P.R.), $5.39 (P.R., dark).

DON Q GOLD (Don Q Imports, Inc., Miami, Fla.), $5.39 (P.R., dark).

RON LLAVE (Compañia Ron Llave, Arecibo, P.R.), $4.71 (P.R., light).

RON CARIOCA WHITE (Schenley Imports Co., N.Y.C.), $5.15 (P.R., light).

BOCA CHICA GOLD ("21" Brands, Inc., N.Y.C.), $5.39 (P.R., dark).

BRUGAL WHITE (Standard Wine & Liquor Co., Inc., N.Y.C.), $4.46 (V.I., light).

PALO VIEJO (McKesson & Robbins, Inc., N.Y.C.), $4.71 (P.R., light).

BOCA CHICA WHITE ("21" Brands, Inc.), $5.39 (P.R., light).

RON BACARDI SILVER (Bacardi Corp.), $5.39 (P.R., light).

RONRICO WHITE (General Wine & Spirits Co., N.Y.C.), $5.35 (P.R., light).

OLD ST. CROIX WHITE (Old St. Croix Importers & Distillers, Boston), $4.35 (V.I., light).

CRUZAN CLIPPER WHITE (Cruzan Imports Co., N.Y.C.), $4.70 (V.I., light).

DON Q WHITE (Don Q Imports, Inc.), $5.39 (P.R., light).

INTERMEDIATE- AND FULL-BODIED RUMS

CU did not carry out taste-tests of intermediate- and full-bodied rums (aside from the full-bodied Puerto Rican item that was hidden among the light-bodied samples), but this capsule discussion may give you some guidelines to follow if you go shopping for an intermediate- or full-bodied brand.

The pungent rums generally associated with Jamaica and certain other places in or bordering on the Caribbean are made in a different way from the light-bodied rums discussed above. The difference starts with the fermentation of the molasses; the skimmings from the sugar barrels (called "dunder" or "burnt ale") are added to impart extra flavor. No yeast cultures are used; instead, the natural yeast spores in the air are allowed to settle on the surface, multiply, and cause fermentation. This is a slow process, taking from five to twenty days and developing many congeners.

The mash is distilled, typically, in a pot still, and the resulting distillate, or "low wine," is redistilled in another pot still to obtain a second distillate known as new rum. This comes off the still at between 140 and 160 proof, or even lower, and is therefore very full-bodied and very rummy. Such full-bodied distillates require longer aging than light rums; those of Jamaica, for example, are usually aged at least seven years. Then, after blending, caramel is added to deepen the color to the shade favored by the producer. This may be anything from a light golden hue to a deep mahogany brown.

Most of these full-bodied rums are bottled at 86 to 97 proof, though some are put up at 151 proof—for flaming or for use in the zombie, a potent drink more popular in the 1940s than now.

A little buying guidance

Rum is made wherever sugar cane is cultivated, but rums imported from outside the Caribbean region are rarely seen in the United States. Products from a few of the rum-producing areas that do export to us are briefly described below. This is by no means a complete survey. Nor—it bears repeating—did CU's experts taste-test these products. Even if they had, many full-bodied rums differ in flavor so sharply from one another that you would still have need to rely on your own taste buds as the final arbiter. Unfortunately, these full-bodied rums are not, by and large, for the economy-minded, so that experimenting with them can be quite costly. More-over, distribution of many of them is limited at best. (Residents of "control" states are at a particular disadvantage in this respect.)

Jamaica

Among rum drinkers, Jamaica is practically synonymous with the dark, heavy, pungent rums it produces. Full-flavored, with colors that range throughout the spectrum of rum hues, these were and perhaps remain the best known of the full-bodied rums. Today, however, Jamaica also turns out large quantities of light-bodied rums, many of them distilled in column stills. Most of Jamaica's production has for a long time been shipped to London in bulk for aging and bottling there; indeed, in England Jamaican rum is sometimes called London Dock rum. Among the comparatively well-known brands of full-bodied Jamaican rums distributed in the United States are Myers's "Planters Punch" ($6.90 at 84 proof) and Hudson's Bay Jamaica ($6.89 at 91.4 proof). Some brands offer "prestige" versions that have been aged for a decade or longer; these may run to about $8 or $10 a fifth.

Demerara, Barbados, and Trinidad

These rums are somewhat—or even considerably—lighter in body than the traditional full-bodied Jamaican products, with which they are sometimes classed as rums of the British West Indies.

Demerara, it should be noted, is not an island or even on one. Instead, Demerara rums take their name from a river that runs through a rich sugar-cane region in Guyana (formerly British Guiana), a small nation on the Caribbean seacoast of South America. Made mostly for export, and typically quite dark in color from generous additions of caramel, Demerara rums are likely to have a less pronounced taste than typical Jamaican rums. Their lighter body stems in part from a much shorter fermentation (three to four days) and distillation, usually, in column stills. Lemon Hart Demerara ($5.75 at 80 proof) and Hudson's Bay Demerara ($6.80 at 91.4 proof) are among brands with some U.S. distribution.

Barbados rums are more likely to be intermediate in color and body than the foregoing products, with a flavor that has been described by some as nearly leathery or smoky. Mount Gay ($7, 90 proof) and Lightbourn's ($6.60 at 92 proof) are among labels that might be found in a few stores.

Trinidad rums tend to be even lighter in body than the other "British West Indies" rums. An example is Siegert's Bouquet Trinidad ($6.75 at 86 proof).

Martinique and Haiti

The "French-speaking" rums produced on these islands are some-what less pungent and lighter in body than the dark Jamaica rums, but not so dry or light-bodied as the usual Puerto Rican product. Martinique's Rhum St. James ($7.43 at 94 proof) is unusual in being made with concentrated cane syrup rather than molasses. It is a rather dark rum with a fruity aroma. Haiti's Rhum Barban-court Reserve Speciale Five Star ($8.45 at 86 proof) is made directly from cane juice. Intermediate in body, it has a quality suitable for sipping as you would brandy. Rhum Barbancourt Three Star ($6.85 at 86 proof) is similar but lighter-bodied and perhaps more popular—for price and for mixing.

United States

American rums are still made, both light-bodied and full-bodied. The so-called "New England" rums are full-bodied products usually distilled at under 160 proof. Until 1968 this designation could be used for a full-bodied rum distilled anywhere in the United States at less than 160 proof. Now, however, it can be applied only to rums actually produced in New England—and the rum can be dis-tilled up to 190 proof. The New England rums are traditional toddy ingredients, and are less pungent or "rummy" than a full-bodied Jamaican rum. The New England states themselves consti-tute the bulk of the market for this rum, an example of which is Old Medford ($4.65 at 86 proof).

~~~~~~

Chapter 13

BRANDIES

Brandy, especially French grape brandy, exists within an aura of legend and ceremony all its own. Its origins were humble enough: distilled wine infusions of herbs and other plant materials, which were used as medicinals in Europe as early as the thirteenth century, many years prior to the coining of the word "brandy" from the Dutch *brandewijn* ("burnt wine"). But then, even before the days of Napoleon and those trusty Alpine St. Bernards, there began to develop a veritable brandy mystique, so that now this liquor is sniffed and sipped and discussed in terms that border on the spiritual. The basics of brandy, however, are actually quite down-to-earth. All brandies are, by law, spirits distilled from fermented fruit.* Any fruit will do—apples, plums, and apricots are used in various countries, for example—but by far the most important brandies are those made from grapes. A product labeled simply *brandy* must always be an unsweetened distilled spirit derived exclusively from fermented grapes—*i.e.,* from wine of grapes. Brandies derived from other fruits must be so labeled; some of those fruit brandies are discussed on page 176. Certain sweetened fruit-flavored cordials may bear the word *brandy* on the label, though only in conjunction with the word *flavored*—e.g., "black-

---

More specifically, U.S. regulations define brandy as "an alcoholic distillate from the fermented juice, mash or wine of fruit, or from the residue thereof, produced at less than 190 proof . . . and bottled at not less than 80 proof." It also must have "the taste, aroma, and characteristics generally attributed to the product."

berry-flavored brandy" (see Chapter 14). This chapter is devoted principally to unflavored grape brandies, which are produced almost everywhere wine is made from grapes. French grape brandies are, of course, the most celebrated and account for more than half of all brandy imported by the United States.

COGNAC

Of all the world's brandies, Cognac is without doubt the most famous, and by reputation the finest. It began to be produced commercially early in the seventeenth century, although it did not come to be called Cognac until much later. Named for a town in the Charente district of western France, it is made from grapes grown solely in an area strictly delimited by French law. Even the United States, which often allows products a wide latitude in the use of place-derived names, agrees that spirits labeled *Cognac* or *Cognac (grape) brandy* must indeed be "grape brandy distilled in the Cognac region of France (the Charente), which is entitled to be so designated by the laws and regulations of the French Government."

The geographic limits of the Cognac region are further demarcated by French regulations into seven subdivisions roughly according to the chalk content of the respective soils. Beginning with the chalkiest area, these are Grande Champagne,* Petite Champagne, Borderies, Fins Bois, Bons Bois, Bois Ordinaires, and Bois Communs. Other things being equal, the more chalk, the better the Cognac.

The other basic requirements that the French have established for Cognac are: (1) double distillation in old-style copper pot stills (which is nearly always done by the small farmer-distillers) and (2) aging for at least two years in casks made of oak from the nearby Limousin Forest, near Limoges.

It is usually the Cognac shippers and blenders who handle the aging, which may continue for as long as fifty years. Very little

---

* *In this usage, the word "champagne" has no connection with champagne, the wine, nor the district in which it is produced.*

brandy, though, is aged for more than, say, fifteen or twenty years. Like many other distilled spirits, Cognac is almost always a blended product. Some "straight" or vintage Cognacs have been made, but it is rare to get a balanced and complete Cognac from one year—and from a single subdivision. From his vast store of Cognacs of various types and ages, the Cognac bottler picks and chooses to achieve a uniformity of flavor and aroma for each of the brands in his line. The blender may use some Cognac from the Borderies area for body, some from Grande Champagne, perhaps, for finesse, some Fins Bois for flavor—and so on, with each selection possibly from a different year.

Types of Cognacs

If you see stars when you look at a Cognac label, don't conclude that they're telling you the number of years that the contents have been aged. According to CU's consultants, the stars merely indicate the shipper's estimation of the quality of his product. The various Cognacs in a "Three Star" brand are likely to have averaged around five years or so in the barrel, those in a "Five Star," somewhat longer, our consultants say. Among the brands submitted to CU's taste tests, those with the stars usually represented the lower end of their line's price range.

Cognacs designated *V.S.O.P.* are generally more costly (and supposedly older and finer) than starred brands, but, like the stars, the initials do little more than identify a *style* of brandy. There is no use hunting for French words to fit them—they stand for English words: Very Superior Old Pale. A brandy labeled *V.S.O.P.* is believed (or at any rate claimed) by its producer to be of the quality signified (though a Frenchman may tell you the letters mean *versez sans oublier personne,* or "pour without forgetting anyone"). Other alphabet-soup designations are *X,* for Extra; *F,* for Fine; and *E,* for Especial.

In an earlier brandy project, CU's technicians, out of curiosity, compared the colors of V.S.O.P. Cognacs with those of starred bottles. The V.S.O.P.s were, if anything, generally darker than the starred brands of the same line. The "Pale" designation, in fact, derives from practices in the British market, where English distributors found that the consumer seemed willing to pay a bit extra for the privilege of enjoying the fine yellow color that well-aged brandies develop. With perhaps characteristic British understatement they called these older brandies "Pale." In the U.S. market the emphasis is on "Old"—and things that are darker evidently look older. Aging spirits in wood causes them to darken, of course, and the addition of caramel will make them, if need be, darker still. A Cognac marked *Nature* has had no sugar or caramel added.

Though the brandies in a given blend may be anywhere from two to fifty years old, under U.S. regulations any age given on the label must be that of the youngest brandy present. Moreover, the French government (upon whose certification the U.S. Treasury Department relies) keeps no records in the Charente of brandy aging that extends beyond five years. So a Cognac producer empowered to label his product either *five years old* (the most he can say) or *V.S.O.P.* (with the aura of prestige) is hardly likely to choose the first alternative.

The words *Grande Fine Champagne* do have a very specific meaning on a label. Under French law, they can be used only on a Cognac produced in the Grande Champagne district. *Fine Champagne* indicates a Cognac produced with grapes from both Grande Champagne and Petite Champagne. No other such terms have any meaning—*Fine Cognac* or *Reserve Cognac* are nothing more than label puffery.

The ghost of Napoleon

Perhaps in order to suggest a hoariness that can't be claimed directly, Napoleon (whether the original emperor or Napoleon III is often unclear) has been impressed into France's brandy-promoting cause. Any label references to Napoleon should be taken with several grains of salt. CU's consultants aver that there is no such thing available as the legendary "Napoleon Brandy," if such is taken to mean brandy as much as 150 years old. Furthermore, there would be little point in having such a product: After about fifty years in wood, brandy begins to acquire an unpalatable woody taste. Cognac in a barrel since the time of either Napoleon would be undrinkable today. And Cognac in a bottle since Napoleonic times would be only as good as it was, and as old as it was, when it went in; once bottled, spirits do not change. In any event, as far as CU's consultants know, no such antique bottlings are to be found in liquor stores.

These facts have not cramped the imaginations of the brandy packagers, however. Courvoisier styles itself "The Brandy of Napoleon," and one of its brands carries a silhouette of the Little Corporal, hand shoved into coat front. Bisquit has a "Napoleon" bottling. St. Rémy, E. Rémy, and Bardinet call themselves Napoleon brandies without further explanation. Martell V.S.O.P. goes them all one better: its bottles display a seal of Louis XIV.

ARMAGNAC

So far as world reputation goes, Armagnac brandy is second only to Cognac. Armagnac is, like Cognac, distilled in a strictly delimited region of France—in this instance, Gers and Landes, the ancient Gascony, in southwestern France, the land of d'Artagnan.

The Armagnac area is, again like the Cognac region, subdivided according to the gradations of quality to be expected. Soil characteristics are a prime criterion: The best Armagnac comes from Bas-Armagnac (here *bas* means lower in altitude—not in quality), which has a generally sandy soil. The next-preferred is Tenareze; and the least-favored is Haut-Armagnac, which has a chalky soil— an advantage to Cognac, but not to Armagnac.

Armagnac is produced by a single distillation process in a wood-fired, continuous variation of the pot still. The resulting spirits "come over" at a lower proof than Cognac, producing a brandy that is reputedly quite fragrant even when young. For drinking, of course, the flavor must still be smoothed and mellowed by aging in wood—specifically, the black oak native to the Armagnac area.

Armagnacs are generally blended, as are most Cognacs, to produce certain types: "Three Star," "V.S.O.P.," "Extra," etc. Vintage Armagnacs are also offered, and the best of them are very highly prized in some quarters. But they are extremely hard to come by.

According to CU's expert tasters, Armagnacs are somewhat drier than Cognacs. Whether you would agree with them—or, for that matter, whether you would prefer Armagnac to Cognac or to American brandy is, finally, a question for your own taste testing. It should be pointed out, though, that the modest sales of Armagnacs in the United States seem to reflect little more than the relative obscurity of these brandies.

OTHER FRENCH BRANDIES

Cognac and Armagnacs are by no means the only brandies made in France, but the labels of the rest distinguish them by no other title than that of *French brandy*. These other Gallic wine distillates generally undergo slightly different processing from that of either of the more renowned varieties; they are aged in oak casks that are French but not necessarily from the forests of Limousin or Gascony; and they are usually lower in price than either of the famous-name brandies.

Although imports are important market factors, over 80 per cent of the brandies consumed in the United States are "homegrown." Most of these are produced in California from grapes grown there. They are usually distilled in column stills and are aged in American white oak barrels. In general, American brandies can be expected to be sweeter and perhaps more grapey than French brandies.

CHOOSING A BRANDY

Though domestic and imported brandies constituted together only about 3½ per cent of the distilled spirits consumed in the United States in 1971, there are more than fifteen domestic and over a hundred imported brands available in this country.

CU's tests

To get a balanced picture of the market, CU included proportionately more imports than U.S. brands in this project. CU's panel of expert tasters sniffed and tasted six U.S. brandies and twenty-two French brandies. Among the latter were seventeen Cognacs and three Armagnacs. Though some Cognacs cost upwards of $30 per fifth, CU left consideration of those to well-heeled connoisseurs; the Cognac brands sampled by CU ranged from about $7 to $14 a fifth. Most were 80 proof.

Since the types and varieties of brandy have such a long-standing reputation for distinctiveness, the panelists were asked to identify, in blind-taste tests, each coded sample as a Cognac, an Armagnac, a non-Cognac French brandy, a U.S. brandy, or an "other" brandy. There were no "others" among our samples; we included the category as a gentle booby trap for the experts. We also asked them to rate and describe the quality and character of each sample's aroma and flavor.

As it turned out, the well-honed palates of the panel were tripped up by the "booby trap" with some frequency; samples were misclassified as "other" about 15 per cent of the time. On average the experts were able to place a sample correctly only 50 per cent of the time—not a very good showing, but considerably better than pure chance.

The panelists did best with Cognacs, identifying them correctly 60 per cent of the time. But the experts identified Armagnacs and French brandies as Cognacs, too (rarely classifying either of them correctly). Even U.S. brandies passed for Cognacs more than 14 per cent of the time—though they were correctly identified as U.S. brandies in 50 per cent of the relevant tastings. It would seem, then, that a brandy's source doesn't make it absolutely distinctive, even to a well-educated taste.

It appeared from the results that the panelists, as a group, preferred Cognacs. CU's statisticians collated the tasters' comments with an eye to finding some sort of definition for that (more or less) unmistakable Cognac character. The few points that emerged tell more about what the pride of the Charente isn't than about what it is: Cognacs were found less sharp than the Armagnacs, less sweet than the U.S. brandies, but far stronger of "personality" than the plain French brandies.

The manufacturers' quality differentiations as indicated on labels —whether by stars, Fine Champagnes, or famous emperors—proved rather difficult to corroborate in CU's blind tastings. Differences between the various Cognacs were not as great as would have been expected from the price differences, either. True, Hine V.S.O.P., the top-ranked brand, was one of the most expensive Cognacs tested, but second-place Otard Special was nearly the least expensive. Among the Cognacs only the bottom-ranked brand received specifically unfavorable comment, and even it—like every other brandy tested of whatever variety—was rated no worse than fair-to-good. Not surprisingly, then, between closely ranked brands in the Ratings the panelists found little to choose.

Preferences among the Armagnacs favored the Bellows Fine Bas distinctly over the Marquis de Montesquiou; Marquis de Caussade fell somewhere between the two. The panelists termed the two non-Cognac, non-Armagnac French brandies rather innocuous and lacking in positive character, but they tended to prefer the flavor of the St. Rémy Napoleon.

The relatively sweet U.S. brandies were found pleasant in flavor and aroma, if lacking in the distinctive character of the Cognacs and Armagnacs. Our panelists preferred the Paul Masson aroma, perhaps because it seemed to them to have more "Cognac character" than the others.

What to buy

If you like Cognac—or want to find out whether you like Cognac or not—take note that runner-up Otard Special cost $7.60, whereas top-rated Hine V.S.O.P. cost $12. Otard Special was judged a Best Buy.

The Armagnacs tested were in the same price range as Otard

Special. The other French brandies and the Americans cost still less. Should your taste run to brandy sours, sidecars, alexanders, and the like, CU recommends that you buy the least expensive brandy you can find, for it isn't likely that you'll be able to detect differences in quality or character when you use brandy in a chilled, mixed drink.

The typical brandy fan, however, considers a straight after-dinner drink with coffee (or without) the capstone of the meal. If you like your brandy this way, we suggest you avoid using the gigantic, balloonlike snifter, an unnecessary affectation. You should be able to hold the glass easily and warm it in one hand (to release the bouquet). Avoid, too, the 1-ounce thimble, since the bouquet is so much a part of enjoying brandy.

To discover whether you can spot that (somewhat) distinctive Cognac or Armagnac character, you might give yourself the test described on page 11. Pit the Cognac and the Armagnac against each other, or pit one of them against a French or U.S. brandy. If you do badly on the test, you may decide that the least expensive brand in the project, the domestic Hartley Six Star ($5.30), is the one for you, whether you sip it straight or not.

Ratings of French and U.S. Brandies

Within types, listed according to the preference of CU's expert tasters for each brandy's aroma and flavor quality. Closely ranked brands differed little in overall quality. All brandies are 80 proof unless otherwise noted; for brandies of other proof, the cost equivalent of an 80-proof fifth is noted parenthetically. Prices are recommended retail per fifth for New York State; prices may differ in other states, but the price relationship among brands should be similar.

COGNACS

HINE V.S.O.P. FINE CHAMPAGNE ("21" Brands, Inc., N.Y.C.), $12.
OTARD SPECIAL (Schenley Import Co., N.Y.C.), $7.60. A BEST BUY.

HENNESSY V.S.O.P. RESERVE GRANDE FINE CHAMPAGNE (Schieffelin & Co., N.Y.C.), $12.80. Good aftertaste.

COURVOISIER V.S. (W. A. Taylor & Co., N.Y.C.), $10.98.

BISQUIT VSOP FINE CHAMPAGNE (Heublein, Inc., Hartford, Conn.), $10.52.

OTARD THREE STAR (Schenley Import Co.), $8.25.* Smooth flavor.

MARTELL V.S.O.P. MEDALLION FINE CHAMPAGNE (Browne-Vintners Co., N.Y.C.), $14.35.

PRINCE HUBERT DE POLIGNAC THREE STAR (Dennis & Huppert, Inc., N.Y.C.), $8.60. 84 proof ($8.19). Light aroma.

OTARD V.S.O.P. (Schenley Import Co.), $10.95.

GASTON DE LAGRANGE THREE STAR (Park, Benziger & Co., Inc., N.Y.C.), $6.79.

REMY MARTIN V.S.O.P. FINE CHAMPAGNE (Renfield Importers, Ltd., Newark, N.J.), $12.55.

PRINCE HUBERT DE POLIGNAC V.S.O.P. FINE CHAMPAGNE (Dennis & Huppert, Inc.), $10.95.

COURVOISIER V.S.O.P. FINE CHAMPAGNE (W. A. Taylor & Co.), $11.26.

MARTELL THREE STAR (Browne-Vintners Co.), $11.25.

DENIS-MOUNIE GOLD-LEAF (Carillon Importers, Ltd., N.Y.C.), $6.96. Light aroma.

HENNESSY BRAS ARME THREE STAR (Schieffelin & Co.), $11.16.

BISQUIT FIVE STAR SAINT MARTIAL (Heublein, Inc.), $8.49. "Doctored" flavor.

ARMAGNACS

BELLOWS FINE BAS THREE STAR (Munson G. Shaw Co., N.Y.C.), $8.29. 84 proof ($7.89).

MARQUIS DE CAUSSADE A.D.C. (Park, Benziger & Co., Inc.), $7.48. 84 proof ($7.12).

MARQUIS DE MONTESQUIOU 3 MOUSQUETAIRES (General Wine & Spirits Co., N.Y.C.), $7.80. 84 proof ($7.43). Full aroma and flavor.

OTHER FRENCH BRANDIES

ST. REMY NAPOLEON (St. Rémy & Cie, Union, N.J.), $6.41. Sweet flavor.

BARDINET NAPOLEON (Carillon Importers, Ltd.), $5.87.

---

*No New York State price available. This Cognac listed at $8.25 in California.

U.S. BRANDIES

PAUL MASSON (Paul Masson Vineyards, Saratoga, Calif.), $5.99. Light flavor.

CORONET VSQ (Brandy Distilling Co., N.Y.C.), $5.90. Sweet flavor.

THE CHRISTIAN BROTHERS (The Christian Brothers of Calif., Reedley, Calif.), $5.97. Sweet aroma and flavor.

HARTLEY SIX STAR (Shewan-Jones, Asti, Calif.), $5.30. Judged to have slight off-taste.

LEROUX DE LUXE (Leroux & Co., Philadelphia), $5.70. Sweet aroma and flavor.

KORBEL THREE STAR (Heck Brothers, Lodi, Calif.), $5.90.

GRAPE BRANDIES
FROM OTHER COUNTRIES

The United States imports grape brandies from a great many countries other than France, though the amounts involved are quite small in some cases. Our principal source, after France, is Spain; behind Spain are, in no particular order, Italy, Portugal, Germany, Israel, Greece, and Yugoslavia.

According to CU's consultants, Spanish brandies are generally full-flavored, earthy, and sweeter than French brandies. Three examples are Pedro Domecq Fundador ($7.25 a fifth), Gonzalez and Byass Soberano ($6.65 a fifth), and Cardenal Mendoza ($17.78 a fifth).

Greek brandies tend to be dark and sweet, with a complex taste derived from resin and other flavorings; Metaxa Five Star ($9.35 a fifth) is one of the more widely distributed brands.

Grape brandies from other countries are not considered to have distinguishing national characteristics, though some may take exception to this generalization. Italian brandies popular in the United States are Stock '84 Gran Reserva ($5.70 a fifth) and Mouquin ($5.75 a fifth). Two other imports suggested by our consultants are Germany's Asbach Uralt ($8.49 a fifth) and Israel's Carmel Richon Le Zion ($7.92 a fifth).

BRANDIES FROM OTHER FRUITS

Applejack

The principal U.S. fruit brandy (not made from grapes) is apple brandy (applejack), most of it made in New Jersey and New York. It has a fine fruity flavor and brown color, and it has usually been aged for several years. In the opinion of CU's consultants, applejack is in general equal in quality to calvados, the well-known French apple brandy, though slightly different in flavor. (Calvados is aged longer and is never blended with neutral spirits, as applejack often is.) A suggested U.S. applejack is Laird's ($5.48 a fifth).

Slivovitz

Slivovitz, a plum brandy, is made throughout Central Europe. It has a fruity flavor with a slight taste of bitter almonds. A good brand to try, in the opinion of CU's consultants, is Braun's Hungarian Kosher Plum Brandy Slivovitz ($7.83 a fifth).

White fruit brandies

These products are called "the white alcohols"—aged in crockery, not in wood, they have no, or virtually no, color. All represent the absolute elixir of the fruit of which they are made. They should not be confused with fruit-flavored liqueurs or cordials (see Chapter 14), though they are often offered on a tray with cordials. The most popular is kirschwasser, made from wild black cherries, but there are also strawberry (fraise), raspberry (framboise), blackberry, and pear brandies. The finest of these come from Switzerland, Alsace, and the Black Forest region of Germany. Also from Alsace come mirabelle and quetsch, brandies made from the yellow plum and blue plum, respectively. All the white fruit brandies are costly to produce because a large quantity of perfect fruit is required to make each bottle, and the fermentation may take as long as a year. They are correspondingly expensive ($12 to $15 for a fifth), but a small amount imparts a great deal of flavor to coffee, a cocktail, a soufflé, or a fruit dessert—ways in which they are often used here. As an after-dinner drink, they should be served icy-cold in a medium-size brandy or tulip glass to capture the unusual bouquet.

~~~~~~

Chapter 14

CORDIALS

There are many different kinds of cordials, or liqueurs—the words are synonymous—but all are distilled spirits combined with flavoring materials, and all are sweet or at least sweetish.* So much for a general description. Within it, cordials can be made by combining just about any natural flavor or flavorings with either neutral spirits or any other spirits—and by a variety of techniques. Most cordials are bottled at between 60 and 70 proof, but some are 50 proof or less, while others are as high as 110 proof. Finally, cordials may be any color, derived either from flavoring materials or from added coloring.

The history of cordials parallels that of early medicine. Even today Webster's defines the word "cordial" as "an invigorating and stimulating medicine, food, or drink." One of the oldest cordial-like products on record, hydromel, was a mixture of wine, honey, and herbs developed by Hippocrates, the father of medicine. Early brandies, too, led to cordial-making, for like the medicines of old, they needed the flavorings of fruits and herbs and what-not to mask their unfortunate taste.

How they're made

Traditionally, cordials have been made by one of three basic

---

* *U.S. Treasury regulations require that cordials contain "sugar, dextrose, or levulose, or a combination thereof, in an amount not less than 2½ per cent by weight of the finished product."*

methods or a combination of them: infusion (or maceration), percolation, and distillation. The infusion method is similar to the making of tea; the percolation method, to the making of coffee in a percolator. Distillation involves distilling a mixture of spirits and fruit or flavorings at a temperature high enough to vaporize the alcohol and the flavoring elements.

These traditional methods are, for the most part, time-consuming and expensive—witness the high cost of many cordials—and are not required by law. Regulations governing cordials permit the direct mixing of distilled spirits with juices or extracts derived from "fruits, flowers, plants, or other natural flavoring materials." Such simple mixing, while it may not capture the essence of the flavor source in quite the same way, can nevertheless result in a pleasant after-dinner drink.

The kinds of cordials

There are, generally speaking, two classes of cordials—the generic type made by many producers and best known by its flavor name (anisette, apricot, crème de menthe, and so on) and the proprietary or brand-name cordial, made by just one producer. In the second group are the secret formulas handed down from generation to generation (Benedictine and Chartreuse are examples). Other proprietary cordials are simply the best-known brands of generic types, as for example, Cointreau, which is a triple sec, and Grand Marnier, which is a curaçao.

Normally included as "cordials" are the fruit-flavored brandies, a group over which some confusion in labeling has arisen. Thus, you will see the term *apricot-flavored brandy* as well as *apricot liqueur* on the cordial shelf at the store. The fruit-flavored brandies (which must be labeled as such) are not, as explained in Chapter 13, *true fruit* brandies, which are natural alcoholic beverages distilled solely from fermented fruit. A *fruit-flavored* brandy is made simply by adding flavoring to any brandy. It must be bottled at 70 proof or more; as a brandy, it does not need to contain 2½ per cent sugar. (In actual practice most fruit-flavored brandies have at least this much sugar if not more.) These fruit-flavored brandies are offered by many U.S. producers (page 189) and are not included in the list below.

It is interesting to note that the words *dry* or *dry liqueur** may be used on the label of a cordial if the sugar content is under 10 per cent. In relation to other truly dry spirits, its use here hardly seems appropriate, since all cordials must have at least 2½ per cent sugar.

General buying advice

CU did not carry out taste-tests of cordials. Each cordial type has its own flavor, which you may or may not like; one type is not necessarily superior in quality to another type, but merely different, just as rum is different from whiskey. While CU's consultants have sought to present a range of cordial types, their survey cannot be considered comprehensive.

Cordials are usually served in small glasses—a sensible practice in view of the high cost of some of them. Prices range from $4 or so per fifth up to $10 or more. Many cordials, however, are available in 1½- to 2-ounce bottles, where permitted under state laws. If you are in a state that allows the sale of these miniatures, you will be able to sample a reasonable number of cordials at a reasonable outlay. This can help you decide which one (or ones) you really want to invest in.

In the listings that follow, the basic flavor used is indicated in most cases and may help you to pick out cordials you would like to try. For most types, general buying advice or specific brand suggestions are given, based on our consultants' judgments. If you are buying a cordial for use primarily in mixed drinks, such as the

---

In some states, much of the "dry liqueur" business consists of half-pint bottles of popular distilled spirits—blends, vodkas, etc.—with 2½ per cent sugar added. This maneuver circumvents those state laws that prohibit half-pint liquor bottles but not half-pint cordial bottles. This is enough extra sweetness to make a perceptible difference in taste if you take your spirit straight, and perhaps even if you drink it with a mixer.

margarita (which uses triple sec) or the stinger (which uses crème de menthe), try the lowest-priced brand first, since the subtleties of flavor are likely to be lost in any case.

Listing of Cordials

This list combines, in alphabetical order, both generic and proprietary cordials. Proprietary names are in italics. Within generic types, the brands listed are those recommended by CU's consultants (but not submitted to taste tests). If the advice is simply to buy a U.S. brand, consult the list of recommended U.S. producers on page 189. Except as noted, the prices are for fifths (25.6 fluid ounces). Where several brands are considered to be of about the same quality, they are listed in order of increasing price per fifth, without regard for differences in proof.

ANISE-LICORICE (OR ANESONE)

Cordials deriving their flavor from a combination of anise and licorice are made in a number of countries under a number of different names. All have a flavor similar to absinthe (now banned in most countries), as well as absinthe's characteristic of turning a milky, opalescent hue when mixed with water. The most famous of these is Pernod Anis, long made in Europe but now also made here; it costs, at 90 proof, $7.45. The famous pastis of Marseilles is now available here: Ricard ($5.81; 90 proof). Other such cordials, generally known as anesones, are made both here and abroad; it is recommended that you try one of the following U.S. brands, all at 90 proof: Nuyens ($4.99); Jacquin's ($5.27); and Leroux ($6.15). Ouzo is the Greek version; one of the major imported brands is Metaxa ($7.59; 90 proof).

ANISETTE

An anise-seed flavored cordial, usually colorless, but sometimes red. The French Marie Brizard ($8.99 for 23.6 fl. oz.; 50 proof) is famous, but may not seem to you to be worth its very high cost. Try first one of the following U.S. brands: Jacquin's ($3.69; 60 proof); Arrow ($4.59; 60 proof); Hiram Walker ($4.63; 60 proof); Leroux ($4.89; 60 proof); Cointreau ($4.93; 50 proof) Garnier ($4.95 for 24 fl. oz.; 54 proof); Bols ($4.98; 50 proof). You might also try, if you like a fairly dry anise cordial, the Spanish Anis del Mono ($7.49 for 24 fl. oz.; 78 proof).

APRICOT

Fruity flavor with an almond undertone. CU's consultants feel that the imported Dolfi ($4.72 for 25 fl. oz.; 42 proof); Cusenier ($6.19; 64 proof); Bols ($8.35 for 25 fl. oz.; 62 proof); and Marie Brizard "Apry" ($8.99 for 23.6 fl. oz.; 70 proof) are superior to the following U.S. brands, all 60 proof: Jacquin's ($4.24); Cointreau ($4.93); Hiram Walker ($5.19); domestic Bols ($5.35); Garnier ($5.55).

BENEDICTINE, D.O.M.

A spicy, aromatic, plant-flavored cordial with a brandy base. It costs $10.89 for 23 fl. oz. at 86 proof. It has been made in France since first created in 1510 by a French Benedictine monk. The initials stand for *Deo Optimo Maximo* ("To God, most good, most great").

B AND B LIQUEUR D.O.M.

A mixture of Benedictine and Cognac, hence drier than Benedictine itself, made by the makers of Benedictine, and sold at the same price and proof. If you prefer a drier cordial with some of the Benedictine flavor, you might try mixing your own, using Benedictine and a brandy of your choice.

BLACKBERRY

U.S. blackberries are as good as European blackberries, and so, generally speaking, are the U.S. cordials; thus you can choose one of the following domestic brands at quite a good saving over the imports: Cointreau ($4.93); Bols ($5.35); Garnier ($5.55). All 60 proof. The imported Cusenier and Marie Brizard are $6.19 and $8.99, respectively.

CHARTREUSE

Spicy, aromatic, plant-flavored liqueurs, having a brandy base, made for centuries at the Monastery of the Grande Chartreuse in France. The green liqueur ($10.49 for 23.6 fl. oz.; 110 proof) is drier than the yellow ($9.74 for 23.6 fl. oz.; 86 proof).

CHERRY

A pleasant cherry flavor with a bitter almond undertone. The most famous brand is Cherry Heering ($10.59 for 24 fl. oz.; 49 proof), made in Denmark from the richly flavored small Danish black cherry. You can get very much the same flavor, though at somewhat lower proof, at less than one-third the price, in several brands of sweet Danish cherry wine. CU's consultants suggest that you try, for ex-

ample, Cherry Kijafa ($3.19 for 24 fl. oz.; 35 proof) even before try-
ing one of the U.S. cherry cordials, such as (all 60 proof): Cointreau
($4.93); Leroux ($5.15); Garnier ($5.55). These do not have the dis-
tinctive Danish cherry flavor. Wishniak ($7.77; 80 proof) is a black
cherry cordial from Poland. See also *Maraschino*.

CHOCOLATE

Vandermint, a minted chocolate from Holland, is used by many to pour
over ice cream. It is $10.25 at 60 proof. A similar product is sold by
De Kuyper as Chocla Menthe ($5; 54 proof), and Hiram Walker
also makes a chocolate-mint cordial ($5.43; 54 proof). Somewhat dif-
ferent is a chocolate-cherry cordial from Switzerland called Cheri-
Suisse ($10.25; 60 proof). See also *Crème de Cacao*.

COFFEE

There are a number of coffee-flavored liqueurs. Especially good are
the Mexican Kahlúa ($8.59; 53 proof) and the rum-based Jamaican
Tía Maria ($9.15 for 23 fl. oz.; 63 proof).

COINTREAU LIQUEUR

See *Triple Sec*.

CRÈME DE BANANE

A sweet banana liqueur, strongly flavored by the fruit. Try first a
U.S. brand, such as Bols ($5.35; 56 proof), before going to such
imports as Marie Brizard ($8.99 for 23.6 fl. oz.; 50 proof).

CRÈME DE CACAO

A chocolate-flavored cordial with a vanilla undertone. The European
producers have to import their chocolate, just as we do. Most U.S.
producers make this cordial; try first any domestic brand, for example
Bols ($5.35; 54 proof). Imports include Cusenier ($6.19; 54 proof)
and Marie Brizard ($8.99 for 23.6 fl. oz.; 50 proof).

CRÈME DE CASSIS

A red, very sweet black-currant cordial of relatively low proof. In
France, it is commonly mixed with vermouth to produce a "vermouth-
cassis" and with dry white wine to make a "kir," both drunk as
aperitifs. Black currants are mostly grown in Europe, so the best of
these cordials are imported. Of the imports, the best are Cartron
($6.16; 38 proof) and Lejay-Legoute ($7.98; 50 proof); and next

best are Cusenier ($5.85 for 24 fl. oz.; 32 proof); Garnier ($8.49 for 24 fl. oz.; 36 proof); and Marie Brizard ($8.99 for 23.6 fl. oz.; 50 proof). A few U.S. producers make this cordial at a much lower price: Dubouchett ($3.35; 35 proof); Leroux ($4.99; 35 proof); Garnier ($5.25; 36 proof).

CRÈME DE MENTHE

A sharp mint-flavored cordial that may be colored green, white, or sometimes pink. CU's consultants feel that U.S. crème de menthes made by most of the producers listed on page 189 are as good as the imports. Choose among them by price; they are usually at or near 60 proof. A recommended import is Get Frères Pippermint ($7.79 for 23 fl. oz.; 54 proof).

CRÈME YVETTE

A violet-flavored-and-colored liqueur. There is only one brand, made in the United States, though more popular in Europe than at home: Jacquin's ($6.36; 65.5 proof). See also Parfait d'Amour.

CURAÇAO

A liqueur with a distinctive orange flavor derived from the dried peel of the green orange grown on the island of Curaçao, and reddish orange or brownish in color. (Triple sec—see page 188—is flavored with the same orange, but is drier, often higher in proof, and always white.) The French Grand Marnier ($11.54 for 23 fl. oz.; 80 proof; made with Cognac) is very expensive but, in CU's consultants' opinion, worth its price. Aside from this brand, some U.S. brands are as good as imports and much cheaper; try one of the following: Garnier ($5.09; 60 proof); De Kuyper ($5.17; 60 proof); and Bols ($5.45; 64 proof) before going to such imports as Hulstkamp & Zoon or Marie Brizard, at $3 to $4 more per bottle.

DRAMBUIE

A spicy Scotch liqueur, made from Highland Scotch malt whiskey, heather honey, and a number of herb flavorings. It is made in Scotland, at 80 proof, and costs $10.69 for 23 fl. oz. The name comes from the Gaelic an dram buidheach ("the drink that satisfies").

FIOR D'ALPI

The name of this yellow-colored Italian liqueur means "Alpine flowers." One brand sold in the United States is Isolabella ($9.25 for 23 fl. oz.; 92 proof).

FORBIDDEN FRUIT

Made in the United States from shaddock, a grapefruitlike citrus fruit, infused in brandy. A proprietary cordial, it is made by Jacquin's ($6.42; 70 proof).

GALLIANO

A spicy plant liqueur from Italy ($10.59; 80 proof).

GOLDWASSER

An anise- and caraway-flavored liqueur, usually very sweet, with flakes of gold floating about. It was originally made in Danzig (now in Poland), and is still sometimes called Danziger Goldwasser. Der Lachs ($6.77 for 16 fl. oz.; 80 proof) and Mercedes ($8.26 for 24 fl. oz.; 70 proof) are imported from Germany; Goldwasser is made in the United States by Bols ($5.49; 60 proof).

GRAND MARNIER

See Curaçao.

IRISH MIST

A spicy liqueur, similar to Drambuie, but made in Ireland with Irish Whiskey and Irish heather honey. Bottled at 80 proof; it costs $10.75 for 23 fl. oz.

KAHLÚA

See Coffee.

KÜMMEL

Flavored with caraway and cumin seeds. The best is Gilka Kümmel ($8.25 for 24 fl. oz.; 86 proof), imported from Germany. Otherwise, try a U.S. brand; almost all U.S. producers have one, ranging from $5 to $6, and usually 60 or 70 proof.

LOCHAN ORA

Liqueur based on Scotch, not unlike Drambuie ($9.95; 70 proof).

MANDARINE

A tangerine-flavored liqueur, golden in color. Imports include Marie Brizard ($8.99 for 23.6 fl. oz.; 50 proof).

MARASCHINO

A cherry cordial with the distinctive flavor of the fresh marasca cherry—not to be confused with the highly processed maraschino cherry used in cocktails. It is colorless with a pleasant cherry flavor. The following U.S. brands are recommended: Bols ($5.49; 70 proof); Leroux ($5.55; 60 proof); Garnier ($5.95; 60 proof).

PARFAIT D'AMOUR

"A rather poisonous-looking liqueur that tastes like melted jelly beans" is the way one of CU's consultants described this sweet purple cordial with flavoring derived primarily from essence of violets. Try the domestic Bols ($4.98; 58 proof) before paying the premium price for imports such as Marie Brizard ($8.99 for 23.6 fl. oz.; 50 proof). If you like Parfait d'Amour, you might also enjoy the less exotically named variation on the violet theme known as Crème Yvette (see page 185).

PERNOD ANIS

See *Anise-Licorice.*

ROCK AND RYE

The basic ingredients of this U.S. cordial—rock sugar candy and rye whiskey—are suggested by the name. Also, it is almost always fruit-flavored, usually with oranges and lemons, but in some brands with cherries, pineapples, or figs as well. You will also find fruit-flavored "crystallized" rock and ryes; this means that the bottles contain sticks of rock sugar. Almost all U.S. cordial producers offer a rock and rye, usually at 48 or 60 proof, and ranging in price per fifth from $4 to $5. Three widely distributed crystallized rock and ryes are Jacquin's ($3.61; 60 proof), Arrow ($4.99; 60 proof), and Leroux Irish Moss ($5.35; 70 proof).

SABRA

This sweet liqueur takes its name from the term applied to native-born Israeli citizens (and products) and its flavoring from that country's Jaffa oranges plus a touch of chocolate. The golden-brown cordial is $10.25 for 24 fl. oz. at 60 proof.

SLOE GIN

This is not a gin (though it may be gin-based), but a cordial with flavoring derived from sloe berries. These are the smallish fruits of the blackthorn bush, a member of the plum family. Usually fairly sweet by itself, sloe gin is the key ingredient of the sloe gin fizz and other drinks. Almost all U.S. producers make a sloe gin, all at 60 proof and all at $4.50-$5, or a little more, per fifth. These are all, in general, about the same quality, so buy by price whichever suits your taste. Try, for example, Cointreau ($4.93) or Bols ($4.99).

SOUTHERN COMFORT

Made of Bourbon whiskey and fresh peaches. It was invented in the United States, and the proprietary brand, at 100 proof, costs $7.11.

STREGA

A spicy, aromatic plant liqueur, imported from Italy. Liquore Strega costs $10.95 for 23 fl. oz. at 80 proof.

TIA MARIA

See *Coffee*.

TRIPLE SEC

With a flavor derived from the same green orange as Curaçao (see page 185), this is colorless and drier. It is also often made at a higher proof. The most famous brand is Cointreau Liqueur, now made in the United States, at 80 proof and costing $8.30 for 24 fl. oz. This brand was originally called Cointreau Triple Sec, but the brand name became so well known that "Triple Sec" was dropped from the label. There are triple secs produced by European firms, but they are more costly, and no better, than the U.S. Cointreau. If its price seems too high, try one of the following U.S. brands: Bols ($4.89; 60 proof); Garnier ($4.95; 60 proof); De Kuyper ($5.73; 80 proof).

VIEILLE CURE

Popular in France, this gold-tinted plant liqueur is made near Bordeaux. An aromatic brandy-based cordial, it is somewhat reminiscent of Benedictine and Chartreuse (though certainly different from either of those unique liqueurs) and costs $9.45 for 20 fl. oz. at 86 proof.

Recommended U.S. Producers

Any brand, imported or domestic, considered by CU's consultants to be outstanding for a specific type of cordial is recommended for that type. Where the suggestion is to buy any U.S. brand, the reader is advised to choose among the following producers who, in the consultants' judgment, produce good generic-named cordials. They are listed alphabetically.

Arrow, Bols, Canada Dry, Cointreau, De Kuyper,
Garnier, Heublein, Hiram Walker, Jacquin, Leroux, Schenley

~~~~~~~~~~~~~~~~~~~~~~~~~~~~~~~~~~

Chapter 15

PREMIXED COCKTAILS AND COCKTAIL MIXES

M uch has been said in the preceding chapters about spirits, but little about the mixed drinks in which a good deal of the spirits Americans buy is consumed. It's been noted several times that, with the addition of ice and a mixer, even clear-cut differences between brands of spirits can blur if not vanish entirely. But what about the quality of the mixed drinks themselves, particularly if those drinks are cocktails—and more particularly yet if they are commercial premixed cocktails or made from the cocktail mixes to which you add your own liquor? CU tested both premixed cocktails and cocktail mixes to see how each group compared with standard homemade cocktails—in quality *and* cost—and, within each group, how the brands compared with each other.

Expert mixologists insist that, for a good cocktail, none but the freshest and best ingredients will do: fresh fruit squeezed on the spot, odd fluids dribbled in with eyedropper precision, pinches of spices and herbs, and so on. These exacting requirements are certainly not met by premixed cocktails and cocktail mixes; on the other hand, no custom-made cocktail can say, as premixed cocktails do: "Pour over ice, or chill and serve." It may be the lazy man's way, but there must be a lot of lazy men (and women) among us, for both the premixed cocktails and the mixes have become popular.

PREMIXED COCKTAILS

Since you don't add even liquor to them, premixed cocktails are the last word in serving ease. Although some thirty different kinds are marketed, over 75 per cent of their sales are accounted for by just five kinds: gin and vodka martinis, manhattans, daiquiris, and whiskey sours. CU bought the leading brands of these five kinds of premixed cocktails for its blind-taste tests.

CU's tests

Our expert spirits tasters were asked to judge each cocktail on the balance of its ingredient blend, on its flavor strength, and on its dryness, sweetness, and acidity (where applicable). Then they were asked to rate its overall quality, using a seven-point scale in which the number one represented the highest ranking and number seven the lowest. We also calculated the costs of the premixed cocktails and compared them with what you could expect to pay for the ingredients of the corresponding homemade drinks.

The results of our tests indicate that, by and large, what you gain in pour-and-serve convenience you lose in both quality and money. The tasters considered none of the premixed cocktails they tested the equal of their fresh-mixed counterparts. Some brands were judged considerably poorer. And, except for one or two low-rated brands, the cost of most of the premixed products turned out to be greater than that of the comparable made-from-scratch cocktails.

The highest scores were achieved by the best-rated daiquiris and gin martinis; one of the former and two of the latter reached the third position on CU's seven-point scale. But most tested daiquiris and gin martinis ended up in the fourth and fifth positions, and one gin martini finished even lower.

None of the whiskey sours or vodka martinis scored as high as the third position, but neither did any score as low as the bottom-ranked gin martini. Among the manhattans, the tasters found few quality differences—and, for that matter, not much quality, either. Seven brands were placed between the fourth and fifth positions on the seven-point scale; the eighth brand, between the fifth and sixth.

COCKTAIL MIXES

Cocktail mixes require you to add your own liquor to the drink (plus water if the mix is in powder rather than liquid form). They are hardly less convenient than the open-and-pour prepared cocktails, and CU's tests indicate that some mixes make a reasonably decent cocktail. And using mixes for some of the more complex cocktails may even save you money.

Compared to the premixed cocktails, these mixes have other virtues, too. You can readily alter the liquor-to-ingredient balance to suit individual tastes—by adding more or less liquor than is called for. And you can probably buy a selection of mixes *plus* your liquor for less than the cost of similar premixed cocktails. Finally, if the mixes are powders, your bar supplies will fit into a more limited space, and what you don't use will keep. CU found cocktails slightly easier to prepare with the powders, especially one drink at a time. The liquids, in most cases, require measuring, and once opened, they don't keep very well, even in the refrigerator.

CU's tests

From the immense variety of mixes available, brands of five cocktails—whiskey sours, daiquiris, bloody marys, margaritas, and mai tais—were chosen for testing. CU selected these not so much because they are popular as because their homemade prototypes all take some effort to prepare. Even the easiest calls for squeezing fruit and adding at least one other ingredient besides the fruit to the liquor.

For these tests, the cocktails made with mixes were compared with a freshly prepared drink, made to a recipe developed in earlier tastings (where it was adjusted until the taste panelists agreed on a standard of excellence).

The tasters were called upon to judge each cocktail's liquor-to-ingredient balance, sweetness, and flavor strength and then to estimate its overall quality in comparison with that of the standard agreed on. Three categories were set up; equal to the standard, slightly poorer than standard, or moderately poorer. (None was found much poorer than standard.)

The whiskey sour mixes made the best showing. The experts found that, of the brands tested, half produced a drink as good as the standard whiskey sour, even though none of them tasted quite *like* the standard. The rest were judged slightly poorer than standard. None of the brands of the other kinds of mixes tested rated better than slightly poorer than standard. The margarita brands did not do so well, all of them being judged slightly-to-moderately poorer than standard. What seemed to be lacking in the margarita mixes was the subtly sweet essence of the triple sec used in the taster's standard margarita. Since the cost of the triple sec (about 11 cents per drink) was also lacking, these mixes would appear to be bargains—if you're willing to settle for something less than the best.

In general, using the mixes would probably save money over the cocktail made fresh at home, but this is hard to pin down simply because the price of fruit varies enormously with season and location.

What to buy

If convenience is your overriding concern, and you're willing to pay a little extra for it, CU suggests your experimenting with the premixed cocktails and the mixes. They *are* convenient. For martinis, either gin or vodka, or manhattans, use the premixed cocktails. For those with important fruit or spice ingredients, use the liquorless mixes. Take the mai tai, for example—we doubt that many readers would want to make their own mai tais, even if they could save money (and they can't). The standard recipe for a mai tai calls for ten ingredients and a steady hand.

In either convenience category, though, bear in mind that the brands the experts liked best may not be the ones you like best. Let your own taste be the judge.

If convenience is not your number one priority—if cost and quality are more important—be your own bartender. If you've been considering buying mixes because your own drinks don't seem up to standard, CU suggests you give yourself another chance as a drink-maker. This time try following the rules and recipes provided below as well as those tucked in among the Ratings for cocktail mixes.

Here are some of the basic rules for cocktail mixing:

1. Use a measuring jigger—accuracy is important.
2. Stir briskly those cocktails that should be stirred, and stir only long enough to mix—approximately seven stirs. (Overstirring dilutes the cocktail with melted ice.)
3. Shake firmly—do not rock—those cocktails that should be shaken.
4. Use *fresh* lemon, lime, or orange juice when it is called for.
5. Always add the liquor last.
6. Never reuse the ice, rinsed or not.

The martini was made for many years as a two-to-one mix, but for many the current preferred recipe calls for six parts gin to one part vermouth—and ten-to-one is not unknown. Add the ice and stir—do not shake. Garnish each glass, if you like, with a twist of lemon, an olive, or a cocktail onion. A vodka martini is made in the same way in the same proportions. Both, of course, are often served on-the-rocks.

The standard manhattan calls for 1½ ounces of blended whiskey with ¾ ounces of sweet vermouth plus a dash of bitters, all stirred together with cracked ice and then strained into a cocktail glass. A maraschino cherry may be added as garnish.

Ratings of Premixed Cocktails

All were considered Acceptable. Listed by types; within types, listed by groups in order of placement on CU's 7-point scale (position given), as judged by CU's expert tasters; within groups, listed in order of increasing cost per ounce of alcohol (given in parentheses). Comments represent a consensus of the tasters' subjective judgments. Except as noted, all came in a 24-fluid-ounce bottle and prices are the suggested retail in New York State; local prices may differ, but in any one store the price relationship among brands should be similar.

GIN MARTINIS

Except as noted, all were judged to be intermediate-to-dry in sweetness and to have moderate-to-strong flavor, well balanced between gin and vermouth.

THIRD POSITION

CALVERT EXTRA DRY MARTINI (Calvert Distilling Co., Baltimore), $4.19 in Calif. (50¢). 70 proof. Judged dry.

HIRAM WALKER'S EXTRA DRY MARTINI COCKTAIL (Hiram Walker & Sons, Inc., Peoria, Ill.), $4.50 (56¢). 67.5 proof.

FOURTH POSITION

SCHENLEY EXTRA DRY MARTINI COCKTAIL (Schenley Distillers, Inc., Lawrenceburg, Ind.), $4.39 (52¢). 70 proof.

HEUBLEIN EXTRA DRY MARTINI (Heublein, Inc., Hartford, Conn.), $4.43 (55¢). 67.5 proof. Judged of intermediate dryness. Citrus-flowery.

THE CLUB EXTRA DRY MARTINI COCKTAIL (The Club Distilling Co., Hartford, Conn.), $1.10 for 8-fl.-oz. can (57¢). 48 proof. Flowery.

FIFTH POSITION

S. S. PIERCE READY-TO-POUR COCKTAILS MARTINI (S. S. Pierce Co., Boston), $2.87 for 25.6-fl.-oz. bottle in Conn.; not available in N.Y. (47¢). 48 proof. Preponderant vermouth flavor.

PARTY TYME EXTRA DRY MARTINI (Party Tyme Products, N.Y.C.), 84¢ for 8-fl.-oz. can (50¢). 42 proof. Moderate-to-mild flavor. Judged watery.

FIFTH-TO-SIXTH POSITION

ICE BOX INSTANT COCKTAIL MARTINI (Federal Distillers, Inc., Cambridge, Mass.), $2.24 (39¢). 48 proof. Judged of intermediate dryness. Dominant vermouth flavor.

VODKA MARTINIS

Except as noted, all were judged to be dry and to have moderate flavor strength.

THIRD-TO-FOURTH POSITION

HEUBLEIN FULL STRENGTH 11 to 1 VODKA MARTINI COCKTAIL (Heublein, Inc.), $4.98 (55¢). 75 proof.

FOURTH-TO-FIFTH POSITION

CALVERT ELEVEN TO ONE VODKA MARTINI (Calvert Distilling Co.), $4.19 in Calif. (47¢). 75 proof. Almost pure alcohol flavor.

HIRAM WALKER'S VODKA MARTINI COCKTAIL (Hiram Walker & Sons, Inc.), $4.50 (63¢). 60 proof.

MANHATTANS

Except as noted, all were judged to be of moderate flavor strength, fairly well balanced between whiskey and vermouth but tending toward vermouth.

FOURTH-TO-FIFTH POSITION

ICE BOX INSTANT COCKTAIL MANHATTAN (Federal Distillers, Inc.), $2.24 (39¢). 48 proof. Judged sweet. Dominant vermouth flavor.

S. S. PIERCE READY-TO-POUR COCKTAILS MANHATTAN (S. S. Pierce Co.), $2.87 for 25.6-fl.-oz. bottle in Conn.; not available in N.Y. (47¢). 48 proof. Judged intermediate between sweet and dry.

CALVERT MANHATTAN (Calvert Distilling Co.), $4.19 in Calif. (58¢). 60 proof. Judged less sweet than any other brand. Balanced flavor tending toward whiskey.

SCHENLEY MANHATTAN COCKTAIL (Schenley Distillers, Inc.), $4.39 (61¢). 60 proof. Judged intermediate between sweet and dry. Balanced flavor tending toward whiskey.

HEUBLEIN FULL STRENGTH MANHATTAN COCKTAIL (Heublein, Inc.), $4.43 (67¢). 55 proof. Judged sweet.

HIRAM WALKER'S MANHATTAN COCKTAIL (Hiram Walker & Sons, Inc.), $4.50 (68¢). 55 proof. Judged intermediate between sweet and dry.

THE CLUB MANHATTAN COCKTAIL (The Club Distilling Co.), $1.10 for 8-fl.-oz. can (69¢). 40 proof. Judged sweet. Dominant vermouth flavor.

FIFTH-TO-SIXTH POSITION

PARTY TYME MANHATTAN (Party Tyme Products), 84¢ for 8-fl.-oz. can (53¢). 40 proof. Judged intermediate between sweet and dry. Mild flavor; considered too weak.

DAIQUIRIS

Except as noted, all were judged to have moderate-to-strong flavor, balanced between rum and citrus and tending in general to be more sour than sweet.

THIRD POSITION

CALVERT DAIQUIRI (Calvert Distilling Co.), $4.19 in Calif. (61¢). 60 proof.

FOURTH POSITION

HEUBLEIN FULL STRENGTH DAIQUIRI COCKTAIL (Heublein, Inc.), $4.43 (70¢). 52.5 proof. Dominant citrus flavor.

HIRAM WALKER'S DAIQUIRI COCKTAIL (Hiram Walker & Sons, Inc.), $4.50 (71¢). 52.5 proof.

FIFTH POSITION

ICE BOX INSTANT COCKTAIL DAIQUIRI (Federal Distillers, Inc.), $2.24 (53¢). 35 proof. Judged sweet.

S. S. PIERCE READY-TO-POUR COCKTAILS DAIQUIRI (S. S. Pierce Co.), $3.53 for 25.6-fl.-oz. bottle in Conn.; not available in N.Y. (57¢). 48 proof. Strong flavor.

SCHENLEY DAIQUIRI COCKTAIL (Schenley Distillers, Inc.), $4.39 (61¢). 60 proof. Moderately strong flavor. Dominant citrus flavor. Judged sweet.

WHISKEY SOURS

Except as noted, all were judged to be of moderate flavor strength, balanced between whiskey and citrus and more sweet than sour.

FOURTH POSITION

CALVERT WHISKEY SOUR (Calvert Distilling Co.), $4.19 in Calif. (58¢). 60 proof.

SCHENLEY WHISKY SOUR COCKTAIL (Schenley Distillers, Inc.), $4.39 (61¢). 60 proof. Strong flavor. Preponderant whiskey flavor. Judged intermediate between sweet and sour.

HEUBLEIN FULL STRENGTH WHISKEY SOUR COCKTAIL (Heublein, Inc.), $4.43 (70¢). 52.5 proof.

HIRAM WALKER'S WHISKEY SOUR COCKTAIL (Hiram Walker & Sons, Inc.), $4.50 (71¢). 52.5 proof.

FIFTH POSITION

ICE BOX INSTANT COCKTAIL WHISKEY SOUR (Federal Distillers, Inc.), $2.24 (53¢). 35 proof. Dominant citrus flavor. Judged sweeter than any other.

Ratings of Cocktail Mixes

All were considered Acceptable. Listed by types; within types, listed by groups in order of estimated overall quality as judged by CU's expert tasters against CU's fresh-made cocktails (comparative rating given); within groups, listed in order of increasing cost of mix per drink (given in parentheses). Number of cocktails containing 1½ fluid ounces of spirits and mixed according to instructions (1 cocktail per packet or cup in the case of dry mixes) are noted. Prices are the average of those paid by CU's shoppers, exclusive of local taxes.

WHISKEY SOUR MIXES

All were judged slightly sweeter and more citrusy than CU's fresh-made standard whiskey sour, and with a slightly weaker flavor. Standard recipe: 3 fl. oz. whiskey; 1 fl. oz. fresh lemon juice; ⅝ tsp. superfine sugar.

EQUAL to fresh-made cocktail

DON THE BEACHCOMBER liquid (Vita-Pakt, Inc., Covina, Calif.), 99¢ for 25.6 fl. oz. 17 cocktails (5.8¢).

BAR-TENDER'S powder (Brady Enterprises, Inc., East Weymouth, Mass.), 79¢ for 12 packets (6.6¢).

PARTY TYME powder (Party Tyme Products, N.Y.C.), 79¢ for 12 packets (6.6¢).

HOLLAND HOUSE powder (Holland House Brands, Inc., Ridgefield, N.J.), 59¢ for 8 packets (7.4¢).

TONIGHT powder (Heublein, Inc., Hartford, Conn.), 59¢ for 6 aluminum cups (9.8¢).

SLIGHTLY POORER than fresh-made cocktail

HOLLAND HOUSE liquid (Holland House Brands, Inc.), 81¢ for 16 fl. oz. 21 cocktails (3.9¢).

PARTY TYME liquid (Party Tyme Products), 86¢ for 24 fl. oz. 16 cocktails (5.4¢).

TAHITI JOE liquid (Tahiti Joe Co., Los Angeles), 99¢ for 25.6 fl. oz. 17 cocktails (5.8¢).

PERFECT HOST powder (Foremost Foods Company, San Francisco), 79¢ for 10 packets (7.9¢).

SCHWEPPES liquid (Schweppes Cocktail Mixers, Ltd., Stamford, Conn.), 66¢ for 3-pack of 4-fl.-oz. bottles. 8 cocktails (8.3¢).

DAIQUIRI MIXES

All were judged slightly poorer in overall quality than CU's fresh-made standard daiquiri, with a balance of rum and citrus nearly the same as the standard, but sweeter than the standard. Except as noted, all were judged to have the same flavor strength. Standard recipe: 1½ fl. oz. light rum; 1 fl. oz. fresh lime juice; ¾ tsp. superfine sugar.

SLIGHTLY POORER than fresh-made cocktail

DON THE BEACHCOMBER liquid (Vita-Pakt, Inc.), 99¢ for 25.6 fl. oz. 34 cocktails (2.9¢).

HOLLAND HOUSE liquid (Holland House Brands, Inc.), 72¢ for 16 fl. oz. 21 cocktails (3.4¢).

PARTY TYME liquid (Party Tyme Products), 88¢ for 24 fl. oz. 16 cocktails (5.5¢). Judged slightly weaker in flavor than the standard.

TAHITI JOE liquid (Tahiti Joe Co.), 99¢ for 25.6 fl. oz. 17 cocktails (5.8¢).

BAR-TENDER'S liquid (Brady Enterprises, Inc.), 79¢ for 12 packets (6.6¢).

PARTY TYME powder (Party Tyme Products), 79¢ for 12 packets (6.6¢).

HOLLAND HOUSE powder (Holland House Brands, Inc.), 57¢ for 8 packets (7.1¢). Judged slightly weaker in flavor than the standard.

SCHWEPPES liquid (Schweppes Cocktail Mixers, Ltd.), 62¢ for 3-pack of 4-fl.-oz. bottles. 8 cocktails (7.8¢).

PERFECT HOST powder (Foremost Foods Co.), 79¢ for 10 packets (7.9¢).

TONIGHT powder (Heublein, Inc.), 59¢ for 6 aluminum cups (9.8¢). Judged slightly weaker in flavor than the standard.

BLOODY MARY MIXES

All were judged equal to CU's fresh-made standard bloody mary in flavor balance and strength, but differed from the standard in other qualities. Standard recipe: 1½ fl. oz. 80-proof vodka; ¾ fl. oz. fresh lemon juice; 3 fl. oz. canned tomato juice; 4 drops Worcestershire sauce; 2 drops Tabasco sauce; dash of table salt (weighed out as ½ gram); twist of peppermill (Malabar pepper weighed out as 60 mg.).

SLIGHTLY POORER than fresh-made cocktail

HOLLAND HOUSE powder (Holland House Brands, Inc.), 59¢ for 6 packets (9.8¢).

HOLLAND HOUSE liquid (Holland House Brands, Inc.), 69¢ for 24 fl. oz. 5 cocktails (13.5¢).

SCHWEPPES liquid (Schweppes Cocktail Mixers, Ltd.), 64¢ for 3-pack of 4-fl.-oz. bottles. 3 cocktails (21.3¢).

MODERATELY POORER than fresh-made cocktail

PARTY TYME liquid (Party Tyme Products), 86¢ for 24 fl. oz. 8 cocktails (10.8¢).

TAHITI JOE liquid (Tahiti Joe Co.), 99¢ for 25.6 fl. oz. 5 cocktails (19.8¢).

MARGARITA MIXES

All were judged slightly-to-moderately poorer in overall quality than CU's fresh-made standard margarita, with a flavor strength equal to the standard, but differing from the standard in other qualities as noted. Standard recipe: 1½ fl. oz. tequila; ½ fl. oz. triple sec; 1 fl. oz. fresh lime juice.

SLIGHTLY-TO-MODERATELY POORER than fresh-made cocktail

DON THE BEACHCOMBER liquid (Vita-Pakt, Inc.), 99¢ for 25.6 fl. oz. 34 cocktails (2.9¢). Slightly sweeter than the standard.

TAHITI JOE liquid (Tahiti Joe Co.), 99¢ for 25.6 fl. oz. 34 cocktails (2.9¢). Slightly more tequila flavor and moderately sweeter than the standard.

PARTY TYME liquid (Party Tyme Products), 89¢ for 24 fl. oz. 16 cocktails (5.5¢). Slightly more citrus flavor than the standard.

PARTY TYME powder (Party Tyme Products), 79¢ for 12 packets (6.6¢). Slightly sweeter than the standard.

HOLLAND HOUSE liquid (Holland House Brands, Inc.), 69¢ for 16 fl. oz. 10 cocktails (6.9¢). Moderately sweeter than the standard.

HOLLAND HOUSE powder (Holland House Brands, Inc.), 59¢ for 8 packets (7.4¢). Slightly sweeter than the standard.

MAI TAI MIXES

All were mixed with light rum only, and differed from CU's fresh-made standard mai tai as noted. Standard recipe: 1¾ fl. oz. light rum; ¾ fl. oz. dark rum; ¾ fl. oz. curaçao liqueur; ¼ fl. oz. grenadine syrup; ¼ fl. oz. orgeat/orzata almond syrup; ¼ fl. oz. fresh lime juice; 1½ fl. oz. fresh lemon juice; 1½ fl. oz. fresh orange juice; 1½ fl. oz. unsweetened canned pineapple juice; ¼ tsp. superfine sugar.

SLIGHTLY POORER than fresh-made cocktail

PARTY TYME powder (Party Tyme Products), 79¢ for 12 packets (6.6¢). Judged slightly more sour and weaker in flavor than the standard.

TAHITI JOE liquid (Tahiti Joe Co.), 99¢ for 25.6 fl. oz. 8 cocktails (12.4¢). Judged slightly fruitier, sweeter, and weaker in flavor than the standard.

MODERATELY POORER than fresh-made cocktail

HOLLAND HOUSE powder (Holland House Brands, Inc.), 59¢ for 8 packets (7.4¢). Judged slightly sweeter and weaker in flavor than the standard.

PARTY TYME liquid (Party Tyme Products), 62¢ for 24 fl. oz. 8 cocktails (7.8¢). Judged slightly sweeter and weaker in flavor than the standard.

DON THE BEACHCOMBER liquid (Vita-Pakt, Inc.), 99¢ for 25.6 fl. oz. 10 cocktails (9.9¢). Judged slightly fruitier and sweeter than the standard.

HOLLAND HOUSE liquid (Holland House Brands, Inc.), 77¢ for 16 fl. oz. 5 cocktails (15.4¢). Judged slightly sweeter than the standard.

~~~~~~

CU's TASTE TESTS
OF TABLE WINES

As indicated in the Introduction, table wines are normally so variable from area to area (and, in many areas, from year to year) that it is very difficult to taste-test a range of wines and expect the results to be applied with any certainty in the future. Compounding the problem of producing a comprehensive buying guide is the hit-or-miss pattern of wine distribution and the inconsistent pricing of wines across the country. With a much more limited goal in mind, CU carried out a series of three pilot projects—on red, white, and rosé table wines—the results of which were reported in CON-SUMER REPORTS for October and November, 1971, and January, 1972, respectively.

The aim of these tastings was to find inexpensive and widely available wines at as high a quality level as possible. In selecting wines to be included, two criteria were observed: (1) That the wine be available for purchase in most cities across the country; (2) That the wine should cost no more than $4 a bottle.* In all, 120 wines were tasted, almost half of them from the United States, the rest from Europe, mostly from France, Italy, and Germany.

In the tests of reds and whites, the wines were subgrouped by flavor characteristics, not by geographical areas, so that, for exam-

---

There were four exceptions to our $4 rule, each an expensive "sleeper" designed to test whether our expert tasters would ferret out wines traditionally accepted as superior. In most cases they did not. Since the prices in this book are adjusted to June 1, 1972, a few additional wines are now listed over $4.

ple, in the tasting of bordeaux-type wines we included California cabernet sauvignons (varietals) and clarets (generics) as well as château-bottled, commune, district, and monopole wines from Bordeaux itself. In the Ratings, the wines are identified by country of origin (by state, for American wines). To learn more about a particular wine, turn to the proper chapter (on reds, whites, or rosés) and look up the discussion of wines from the country, region, or district named.

The tastings were similar to the others on which the Ratings in this book are based. We assembled a panel of experts and presented them with coded glasses of wine for comparative judging. Each panelist tasted no more than five wines at a sitting, but there were enough sessions so that each man tasted every wine in the group at least twice. The panelists were asked to rate the overall quality of every sample—on CU's poor-to-fair-to-good-to-very-good scale—and to note also the wine's body and dryness.

In general, though all the wines were found drinkable, our testers found few they consistently liked. On the whole, the imported wines were preferred, but some imports were disappointing, and some low-priced domestics were judged as good as or better than august vintages from abroad. Since taste is such an individual matter, these Ratings should be considered merely a starting point for the development of your own preferences in the wide world of wines.

Ratings of Reds, Whites, and Rosés

Within each wine type, listed by groups in order of estimated overall quality, based on the combined judgments of a panel of expert tasters; within groups, listed in order of increasing price; if prices are identical, listed alphabetically. Comments on body and dryness are given only where substantially different from the average for the group. With foreign wines, name in parentheses is that of U.S. importer; with U.S. wines, that of the manufacturer or distributor. Prices are suggested retail in New York State as of June 1, 1972.

Red Wines

BORDEAUX AND BORDEAUX-TYPE WINES

ACCEPTABLE—Good-to-Very Good

PAUL MASSON CABERNET SAUVIGNON (Paul Masson Vineyards, Saratoga, Calif.), $2.79 for 25.6 fl. oz. California.

B&G MÉDOC 1966 (Browne Vintners, N.Y.C.), $3.19 for 24.5 fl. oz. France.

B&G ST. ÉMILION 1966 (General Wine & Spirits Co., N.Y.C.), $3.25 for 24.5 fl. oz. France.

CRUSE LA DAME ROUGE MÉDOC 1966 (The Jos. Garneau Co., N.Y.C.), $3.59 for 24.5 fl. oz. France.

ACCEPTABLE—Good

THE CHRISTIAN BROTHERS SELECT NAPA VALLEY CABERNET SAUVIGNON (The Christian Brothers, Napa, Calif.), $2.85 for 25.6 fl. oz. California.

SICHEL MÉDOC "RUBAN ROUGE" 1967 (Schieffelin & Co., N.Y.C.), $3.19 for 24 fl. oz. France.

LOUIS M. MARTINI CABERNET SAUVIGNON 1966 (Louis M. Martini, St. Helena, Calif.), $3.20 for 25.6 fl. oz. California.

SICHEL ST. ÉMILION 1966 (Schieffelin & Co.), $3.39 for 24 fl. oz. France. Relatively dry.

BEAULIEU VINEYARD NAPA VALLEY CABERNET SAUVIGNON 1966 (Beaulieu Vineyard, Rutherford, Calif.), $3.41 for 25.6 fl. oz. California.

CRUSE LA GARDERIE ST. ÉMILION 1966 (The Jos. Garneau Co.), $3.79 for 24.5 fl. oz. France.

GINESTET MARGAUX 1966 (Kobrand Corp., N.Y.C.), $4.39 for 24 fl. oz. France.

CHANSON CHÂTEAU LA GARDE GRAVES 1966 (Julius Wile Sons & Co., Inc., N.Y.C.), 5.35 for 24.5 fl. oz. France. Relatively dry.

CHÂTEAU LAFITE-ROTHSCHILD 1964 (Monsieur Henri Wines, Ltd., N.Y.C.), $45 for 24 fl. oz. France.

ACCEPTABLE—Fair

ALMADÉN CALIFORNIA MOUNTAIN RED CLARET (Almadén Vineyards, Los Gatos, Calif.), $1.59 for 25.6 fl. oz. California. Relatively light-bodied.

LAVERGNE PAVILLON ROUGE DE BORDEAUX 1966 (Frederick Wildman & Sons, N.Y.C.), $2.55 for 24 fl. oz. France. Relatively light-bodied. Relatively dry.

BURGUNDY AND BURGUNDY-TYPE WINES

ACCEPTABLE—Fair-to-Good

GALLO PAISANO (Ernest and Julio Gallo, Modesto, Calif.), $1.15 for 25.6 fl. oz. California. Less dry than most.

GALLO HEARTY BURGUNDY (Ernest and Julio Gallo), $1.25 for 25.6 fl. oz. California. Less dry than most.

TAYLOR BURGUNDY (The Taylor Wine Co., Inc., Hammondsport, N.Y.), $1.85 for 25.6 fl. oz. New York.

THE CHRISTIAN BROTHERS BURGUNDY (The Christian Brothers), $2 for 25.6 fl. oz. California. Relatively dry.

MIRASSOU SANTA CLARA BURGUNDY (Mirassou Vineyards, San Jose, Calif.), $2.49 for 25.6 fl. oz. California.

WILDMAN PAVILLON ROUGE DU RHÔNE 1967 (Kelley Barton, Ltd., N.Y.C.), $2.75 for 25 fl. oz. France. Relatively dry.

WENTE BROS. GAMAY BEAUJOLAIS 1967 (Wente Bros., Livermore, Calif.), $2.80 for 25.6 fl. oz. California.

WILDMAN BEAUJOLAIS SUPERIEUR LATOUR 1969 (Kelley Barton, Ltd.), $3.15 for 25 fl. oz. France.

LOUIS M. MARTINI MOUNTAIN PINOT NOIR 1966 (Louis M. Martini), $3.20 for 25.6 fl. oz. California.

BEAUJOLAIS LOUIS JADOT 1969 (Kobrand Corp.), $3.69 for 24 fl. oz. France.

CRUSE BEAUJOLAIS 1969 (The Jos. Garneau Co.), $3.69 for 24.5 fl. oz. France. Relatively dry.

CHANSON BEAUJOLAIS ST. VINCENT (Julius Wile Sons & Co., Inc.), $3.75 for 24.5 fl. oz. France. Relatively dry.

F. CHAUVENET CHÂTEAUNEUF DU PAPE 1967 (Austin, Nichols & Co., Inc., N.Y.C.), $5.59 for 25 fl. oz. France. Relatively full-bodied.

GEVREY-CHAMBERTIN CLOS-ST. JACQUES 1962 (Frank Schoonmaker, N.Y.C.), $12 for 24 oz. France. Relatively full-bodied. Relatively dry.

ACCEPTABLE—Poor-to-Fair

ROMA BURGUNDY (Roma Wine Co., Fresno, Calif.), $1.15 for 25.6 fl. oz. California. Relatively light-bodied. Less dry than most.

ITALIAN AND ITALIAN-TYPE WINES

ACCEPTABLE—Good

BROLIO CHIANTI CLASSICO 1966 (Browne Vintners), $3.25 for 32 fl. oz. Italy. (Equivalent to $2.44 for 24 fl. oz.)

SODERI CHIANTI CLASSICO 1964 (Banfi Prod. Corp., N.Y.C.), $2.89 for 24 fl. oz. Italy. Relatively dry.

BOLLA VALPOLICELLA 1966 (Fontana Hollywood Corp., N.Y.C.), $3.75 for 32 fl. oz. Italy. (Equivalent to $2.99 for 24 fl. oz.)

VILLA ANTINORI CHIANTI CLASSICO 1967 (Julius Wile Sons & Co., Inc.), $3.49 for 24 fl. oz. Italy.

ACCEPTABLE—Fair-to-Good

FOLONARI VALPOLICELLA 1966 (Schieffelin & Co.), $2.60 for 24 fl. oz. Italy.

MELINI CHIANTI CLASSICO 1966 (Renfield Importers, Ltd., Union, N.J.), $3.99 for 32 fl. oz. Italy. (Equivalent to $2.99 for 24 fl. oz.)

RUFFINO RISERVA DUCALE CHIANTI 1964 (Schieffelin & Co.), $4.49 for 24 fl. oz. Italy.

ACCEPTABLE—Poor-to-Fair

GALLO CHIANTI (Ernest and Julio Gallo), $1.15 for 25.6 fl. oz. California. Less dry than most.

ITALIAN SWISS COLONY CHIANTI (Italian Swiss Colony, ISC, Calif.), $1.15 for 25.6 fl. oz. California. Less dry than most.

I. L. RUFFINO CHIANTI 1966 (Schieffelin & Co.), $3.75 for 32 fl. oz. Italy. (Equivalent to $2.82 for 24 fl. oz.)

NEW YORK STATE WINES

ACCEPTABLE—Fair-to-Good

BOORDY VINEYARDS RED WINE 1969 (Boordy Vineyards, Westfield, N.Y.), $1.89 for 25.6 fl. oz. New York. Limited supply. Relatively dry.

ACCEPTABLE—Poor-to-Fair

WIDMER NAPLES VALLEY RED (Widmer's Wine Cellars, Inc., Naples, N.Y.), $1.85 for 25.6 fl. oz. New York.

GREAT WESTERN BACO NOIR BURGUNDY (Pleasant Valley Wine Co., Hammondsport, N.Y.), $2.25 for 25.6 fl. oz. New York. Relatively full-bodied. Relatively dry.

ACCEPTABLE—Poor

TAYLOR LAKE COUNTRY RED (The Taylor Wine Co., Inc.), $1.85 for 25.6 fl. oz. New York. Very much less dry than most.

GREAT WESTERN PLEASANT VALLEY RED WINE 1968 (Pleasant Valley Wine Co.), $2.25 for 25.6 fl. oz. New York. Very much less dry than most.

PROPRIETARY VINIFERA WINES

ACCEPTABLE—Fair-to-Good

BODEGAS BILBAINAS VINA POMAL 1964 (Briones & Co., N.Y.C.),

$2.35 for 24 fl. oz. Spain.

GRAO VASCO DAO (Dreyfus, Ashby & Co., N.Y.C.), $2.55 for 25 fl. oz. Portugal.

ACCEPTABLE—Fair

GUILD VINO DA TAVOLA RED (Guild Wine Co., Lodi, Calif.), $1.15 for 32 fl. oz. California.

FAMIGLIA CRIBARI VINO ROSSO DA PRANZO (B. Cribari & Sons, San Francisco), 1.25 for 32 fl. oz. California. Relatively full-bodied.

PAUL MASSON RUBION (Paul Masson Vineyards), $2.10 for 25.6 fl. oz. California.

White Wines

BORDEAUX

ACCEPTABLE—Good

SICHEL GRAVES SUPERIEURES "BONNE TERRE" 1967 (Schieffelin & Co., N.Y.C.), $2.69 for 24 fl. oz. French. Relatively sweet.

ACCEPTABLE—Fair

LAVERGNE PAVILLON BLANC DE BORDEAUX 1967 (Kelley Barton, Ltd., N.Y.C.), $1.99 for 24 fl. oz. French. Relatively sweet.

B&G PRINCE BLANC (Browne Vintners, N.Y.C.), $2.85 for 24.5 fl. oz. French.

CRUSE GRAVES 1967 (The Jos. Garneau Co., N.Y.C.), $2.95 for 24.5 fl. oz. French.

CHANSON CHÂTEAU OLIVIER 1966 (Julius Wile Sons & Co., Inc., N.Y.C.), $4.49 for 24.5 fl. oz. French.

BURGUNDY AND BURGUNDY-TYPE WINES

ACCEPTABLE—Fair-to-Good

GALLO CHABLIS BLANC (Gallo Vineyards, Modesto, Calif), $1.25 for 25.6 fl. oz. California. Relatively light-bodied and sweet.

THE CHRISTIAN BROTHERS CHABLIS (The Christian Brothers, Napa, Calif.), $2 for 25.6 fl. oz. California.

WENTE BROS. PINOT BLANC 1968 (Wente Bros., Livermore, Calif.), $2.80 for 25.6 fl. oz. California.

WENTE BROS. PINOT CHARDONNAY 1967 (Wente Bros.), $3.50 for 25.6 fl. oz. California. Relatively full-bodied.

CHABLIS ALBERT PIC & FILS 1969 (Kobrand Corp., N.Y.C.), $4.19 for 24 fl. oz. French.

L. K. POUILLY-FUISSÉ 1969 (Leonard Kreusch Inc., North Bergen, N.J.), $4.89 for 24 fl. oz. French. Relatively dry.

ACCEPTABLE—Fair

ALMADÉN MOUNTAIN WHITE CHABLIS (Almadén Vineyards, Los Gatos, Calif.), $1.59 for 25.6 fl. oz. California. Relatively light-bodied.

CHABLIS GRAND CRU LES CLOS 1967 (Frank Schoonmaker Importers, N.Y.C.), $5.25 for 24 fl. oz. French. Relatively light-bodied.

ACCEPTABLE—Poor-to-Fair

ITALIAN SWISS COLONY GOLD MEDAL RESERVE CHABLIS (Italian Swiss Colony, Calif.), $1.15 for 25.6 fl. oz. California. Relatively light-bodied and sweet.

B&G PRINCE D'ARGENT (Browne Vintners Co., N.Y.C.), $2.98 for 24 fl. oz. French. Relatively full-bodied and dry.

GERMAN AND GERMAN-TYPE WINES

ACCEPTABLE—Good-to-Very Good

DOPFF VIN FIN D'ALSACE GEWURZTRAMINER 1966 (Carillon Importers, Ltd., N.Y.C.), $4.05 for 24 fl. oz. French (Alsatian). Relatively full-bodied and sweet. Limited supply.

ACCEPTABLE—Good

ALMADÉN GREY RIESLING (Almadén Vineyards), $2.14 for 25.6 fl. oz. California. Relatively dry.

FRANZ WEBER ZELLER SCHWARZE KATZ RIESLING 1969 (Monsieur Henri Wines, Ltd., N.Y.C.), $2.29 for 23.5 fl. oz. German. Relatively light-bodied.

JULIUS KAYSER LIEBFRAUMILCH GLOCKENSPIEL 1967 (Browne Vintners), $3.20 for 23.5 fl. oz. German. Relatively sweet.

LOUIS M. MARTINI MOUNTAIN GEWURZ TRAMINER 1969 (Louis M. Martini, St. Helena, Calif.), $3.20 for 25.6 fl. oz. California.

DEINHARD HANNS CHRISTOF LIEBFRAUMILCH 1967 (Julius Wile Sons & Co., Inc.), $3.30 for 23 fl. oz. German.

BLUE NUN LIEBFRAUMILCH 1968 (Schieffelin & Co.), $3.49 for 23 fl. oz. German.

BLUE NUN BERNKASTELER RIESLING (Schieffelin & Co.), $3.69 for 23 fl. oz. German. Relatively light-bodied.

ACCEPTABLE—Fair-to-Good

LANGENBACH LIEBFRAUMILCH MEISTER-KRONE 1967 (Kelley Barton, Ltd.), $2.85 for 24 fl. oz. German. Relatively light-bodied.

CHARLES KRUG JOHANNISBERG RIESLING (Charles Krug Winery,

St. Helena, Calif.), $3.20 for 25.6 fl. oz. California.

ANHEUSER-BERNKASTELER RIESLING 1969 (The Jos. Garneau Co.), $4.19 for 23 fl. oz. German. Relatively light-bodied.

BERNKASTELER DOCTOR U. GRABEN AUSLESE 1966 ORIGINAL-KELLERABZUG UWE. DR. H. THANISCH (more than one importer and more than one price), $10 to $17.50 for the 23.5 fl.-oz. bottles CU purchased. German. Relatively sweet.

ACCEPTABLE—Fair

GALLO RHINE WINE (Gallo Vineyards), $1.15 for 25.6 fl. oz. California. Relatively light-bodied.

GREAT WESTERN DUTCHESS RHINE WINE (Pleasant Valley Wine Co., Hammondsport, N.Y.), $2.12 for 25.6 fl. oz. New York.

ACCEPTABLE—Poor-to-Fair

PAUL MASSON JOHANNISBERG RIESLING (Paul Masson Vineyards, Saratoga, Calif.), $3 for 25.6 fl. oz. California. Relatively light-bodied and dry.

MISCELLANEOUS WHITE WINES

ACCEPTABLE—Fair-to-Good

BOORDY VINEYARDS WHITE WINE (DRY) 1969 (Boordy Vineyards, Westfield, N.Y.), $1.89 for 25.6 fl. oz. New York. Limited supply.

WENTE BROS. DRY SEMILLON (Wente Bros.), $2.20 for 25.6 fl. oz. California. Relatively full-bodied.

ACKERMAN-LAURANCE POUILLY BLANC FUME 1969 (Kelley Barton, Ltd.), $3.75 for 25 fl. oz. French. Relatively dry.

ACCEPTABLE—Fair

GALLO SAUTERNE (Gallo Vineyards), $1.15 for 25.6 fl. oz. California.

TAYLOR LAKE COUNTRY WHITE (The Taylor Wine Co., Inc., Hammondsport, N.Y.), $1.85 for 25.6 fl. oz. New York. Relatively sweet.

PAUL MASSON EMERALD DRY (Paul Masson Vineyards), $2.10 for 25.6 fl. oz. California. Relatively light-bodied.

BODEGAS BILBAINAS CEPA DE ORO 1964 (Briones & Co., Inc., N.Y.C.), $2.32 for 24 fl. oz. Spanish.

BOLLA SOAVE 1967 (The Jos. Garneau Co.), $3.25 for 24 fl. oz. Italian.

ACCEPTABLE—Poor-to-Fair

ITALIAN SWISS COLONY GOLD MEDAL RESERVE SAUTERNE (Italian Swiss Colony), $1.15 for 25.6 fl. oz. California.

CASAL GARCIA VINHO VERDE BRANCO (Dreyfus, Ashby & Co., N.Y.C.), $2.45 for 25 fl. oz. Portuguese.

MARQUES DE MURRIETA WHITE RIOJA WINE 1961 (Monsieur Henri Wines, Ltd.), $2.99 for 24 fl. oz. Spanish.

ACCEPTABLE—Poor

ROMA'S PRIDE OF THE VINEYARD VINO BIANCO (Roma Wine Co., Fresno, Calif.), $2.09 for 64 fl. oz. (Equivalent to 86¢ for 25.6 fl. oz.) California. Relatively light-bodied.

WINEMASTERS' SAUTERNE (Guild Wine Co., Lodi, Calif.), $1.15 for 25.6 fl. oz. California.

WIDMER LAKE NIAGARA (Widmer's Wine Cellars, Inc., Naples, N.Y.), $1.95 for 25.6 fl. oz. New York. Sweetest white wine tasted.

MELINI ORVIETO SECCO 1968 (Renfield Importers, Ltd., Union, N.J.), $2.99 for 24 fl. oz. Italian.

Rosé Wines

ACCEPTABLE—Fair-to-Good

BLANCHARD ROSÉ D'ANJOU DRY 1969 (Monsieur Henri Wines, Ltd., N.Y.C.), $1.98 for 24 fl. oz. French. Driest of all rosés tasted.

THE CHRISTIAN BROTHERS NAPA ROSÉ (The Christian Brothers, Napa, Calif.), $2 for 25.6 fl. oz. California. Relatively full-bodied.

LOUIS M. MARTINI MOUNTAIN GAMAY ROSÉ (Louis M. Martini, St. Helena, Calif.), $2.20 for 25.6 fl. oz. California. Relatively dry.

NECTAROSE VIN ROSÉ D'ANJOU (Browne Vintners, N.Y.C.), $2.59 for 24 fl. oz. French.

WILDMAN PAVILLON ROSÉ DU RHÔNE 1968 (Kelley Barton, Ltd., N.Y.C.), $2.75 for 25 fl. oz. French. Relatively dry.

MÁTEUS ROSÉ (Dreyfus, Ashby & Co., N.Y.C.), $2.89 for 25 fl. oz. Portuguese.

SICHEL TAVEL PAVILLON DE LA ROSÉ RHÔNE WINE 1967 (Schieffelin & Co., N.Y.C.), $3.59 for 24 fl. oz. French. Relatively dry.

CRUSE TAVEL 1967 (The Jos. Garneau Co., N.Y.C.), $3.89 for 24.5 fl. oz. French. Relatively dry.

LANCERS VIN ROSÉ 1968 (Heublein, Inc., Hartford, Conn.), $3.80 for 25.6 fl. oz. Portuguese.

ACCEPTABLE—Fair

GALLO PINK CHABLIS (Ernest & Julio Gallo, Modesto, Calif.), $1.25 for 25.6 fl. oz. California. Relatively sweet.

TAYLOR ROSÉ (The Taylor Wine Co., Inc., Hammondsport, N.Y.), $1.85 for 25.6 fl. oz. New York State. Relatively dry.

PAUL MASSON VIN ROSÉ SEC (Paul Masson Vineyards, Saratoga, Calif.), $1.89 for 25.6 fl. oz. California. Relatively dry.

ALMADÉN GRENACHE ROSÉ (Almadén Vineyards, Los Gatos, Calif.), $1.92 for 25.6 fl. oz. California. Relatively dry.

GREAT WESTERN ROSÉ (Pleasant Valley Wine Co., Hammondsport, N.Y.), $1.95 for 25.6 fl. oz. New York State. Relatively sweet.

LAVERGNE PAVILLON ROSÉ SELECT 1967 (Kelley Barton, Ltd.), $1.99 for 24 fl. oz. French. Relatively dry.

RUFFINO ROSATELLO (Schieffelin & Co.), $2.69 for 32 fl. oz. Italian. (Equivalent to $2.02 for 24 fl. oz.). Relatively dry.

BEAULIEU VINEYARD BV BEAUROSÉ (Beaulieu Vineyard, Rutherford, Calif.), $2.09 for 25.6 fl. oz. California. Relatively dry.

CRUSE DAME ROSÉ (The Jos. Garneau Co.), $2.79 for 25 fl. oz. French.

OLIVIER CHÂTEAU D'AQUERIA PREMIER GRAND CRU TAVEL ROSÉ 1969 (Kobrand Corp., N.Y.C.), $3.49 for 24 fl. oz. French. Relatively dry.

ACCEPTABLE—Poor-to-Fair

ITALIAN SWISS COLONY GRENACHE VIN ROSÉ (Italian Swiss Colony, Calif.), $1.15 for 25.6 fl. oz. California. Relatively full-bodied and relatively sweet.

PETRI GRENACHE VIN ROSÉ (Petri Wineries, San Francisco), $1.15 for 25.6 fl. oz. California. Relatively full-bodied and relatively sweet.

GOLD SEAL WINE ROSÉ (Gold Seal Vineyards, Inc., Hammondsport, N.Y.), $1.85 for 25.6 fl. oz. New York State. Relatively full-bodied and relatively dry.

WIDMER LAKE ROSELLE (Widmer's Wine Cellars, Inc., Naples, N.Y.), $1.95 for 25.6 fl. oz. New York State. Relatively light-bodied and sweetest of all rosés tasted.

MEIER'S ISLE ST. GEORGE ROSÉ (Meier's Wine Cellars, Inc., Silverton, Ohio), $2.19 for 25.6 fl. oz. Ohio. Relatively full-bodied.

CHÂTEAU STE. ROSELINE (Julius Wile & Sons & Co., N.Y.C.), $3.59 for 25 fl. oz. French. Relatively dry.

INDEX